a single,
numberless death

Nora Strejilevich

a single,
numberless death

Translated from the Spanish by Cristina de la Torre
with the collaboration of the author

University of Virginia Press • Charlottesville and London

Originally published in Spanish as *Una sola
muerte numerosa* by the North-South Center Press,
Miami, Florida, 1997.

University of Virginia Press
© 2002 by the Rector and Visitors of the
University of Virginia
All rights reserved
Printed in the United States of America on
acid-free paper
First published 2002

9 8 7 6 5 4 3 2 1

Library of Congress Cataloging-in-Publication Data
Strejilevich, Nora.
  [Sola muerte numerosa. English]
  A single, numberless death / Nora Strejilevich ;
translated from the Spanish by Cristina de la Torre
with the collaboration of the author.
    p.   cm.
Includes bibliographical references.
  ISBN 0-8139-2130-9 (cloth : alk. paper) —
ISBN 0-8139-2131-7 (pbk. : alk. paper)
  I. De la Torre, Cristina.   II. Title.
  PQ6669.T74 S6513 2002
  863' .64—dc21
                                        2001007449

From 1975 on, my entire country metamorphosed into a single, numberless death. At first this seemed intolerable, but later it was accepted with indifference and even relegated to oblivion.

—Tomás Eloy Martínez, *Lugar común la muerte*

For those who told me their lives far into the night and offered me the gift of stories in moments long as years.

For those who helped me by reading, or simply by being.

For the three of you whose departure left me in mid-sentence.

Contents

- tyranny → cruel gov.
- perverse → acting out expected (wrong)
- exorcise → get rid of, expel (evil, sin)
- cyclone → large scale mass (like hurricane)
- amid → in the background
- reverberate → repeat several times (echos)
- precarious → uncertain
- splotch → smeared
- quiver → tremble / shake
- scold / reprimad → angry rebulce = expression sharp dissapproval.
- mutilate → seriously damaged
- embroider → design thread.
- endearment → love, affection.
- eccentric → strange, uncommon.
- aquiline → like eagle (beak)
- agitator → trouble maker.
- pristine → orginal condition, new fresh.
- dement → mark award for fault / offense

Foreword

There are certain events in Latin American history, such as the neofascist tyranny experienced from the mid-1960s to the mid- to late 1980s, that result in their own unique forms of cultural production. These forms refer to the experience of living under state terror and of undergoing the effects of neofascism, from generalized experiences of repression to the cycle of arrest, detention, interrogation, torture, disappearance, and exile. In the case of Argentina, this spectrum has produced a considerable bibliography of literary works in the form of short stories, poetry, song, novels, and theater, as well as a vast body of essays, journalistic reporting, sociopolitical investigations, and historical interpretations. And it has produced an impressive cinematographic record, from Luis Puenzo's *La historia oficial* (1985), the only Latin American film ever to win an Oscar, to Marco Bechis's *Garage Olimpo* (1999).

Nora Strejilevich's novel originally appeared in Spanish in 1997, published by the North-South Center of the University of Miami as part of its Letras de Oro prize competition. This is not the place to contextualize Strejilevich's narrative by evoking the bibliography of Argentine texts alongside which it takes its place. There are simply too many, and there is little to be gained by praise through affiliation or juxtaposition. Nevertheless, a few comments of characterization are in order. For example, Spanish is a Latinate language characterized by a certain periodic density that can be enormously problematic for a translation into English. Such periodic writing marks the privileged domain of liter-

ature and signals the difference between an automatized colloquial speech and the specialized métier that literature is con-
ceived to be. Thus, it is striking to note the apparently facile language of Strejilevich's novel, the conscious effort to reproduce
colloquial speech, and the way actual testimony intermingles
with the poetic voice of the narrator. But what is even more
crucial is the way in which her narrative captures the fear, the
terror, and the psychological disengagement that renders the
measured rhythms of educated or erudite expression wholly in-
adequate.

The text is both fictional and documentary. It is fictional in
that it attempts to tell a story that is not that of a specific historical individual but rather that of individuals who are figures of an
entire national social and political experience. It is documentary
in that it is driven by specifically systematized information now
widely available in official and authoritative sources about the
processes of repression, about the ordeal of those who actually
became victims of state terrorism. But more important are the
enormous lacunae that separate the events being narrated from
what one considers to be everyday normality in a putatively civilized society. What appears to be a facilely driven sequence of
events becomes unreal, fantastic, surreal, grotesque in the sheer
unimaginableness of what is being narrated so forthrightly.

Finally, all of these narratives are marked by the obsession to
tell the one macro-narrative of human existence under very contemporary conditions of absolute terror. The psychological and
physical traces of terror remain today in a country that has not
yet come to terms with its past or with the abiding institutions
that led to the immediate past and to an ongoing historical present: Argentina has yet to address the entrenched dynamics of au-
thoritarianism, even under democracy; has yet to resolve a history of anti-Semitism; has yet to acknowledge a history of sexist
oppression; has yet to engage with a culture of difference.

These narratives remain valid today as exemplars of the profound need of one nation to come to terms with the nightmare of history. They remain valid as well because they tell stories that still haunt the Argentine imagination. These narratives are always contemporary because there is no absolute guarantee that the same horror will not be repeated again, and with exactly the same details of plot and action.

David William Foster
Phoenix, August 2001

Acknowledgments

Without what happened to us after 1976

Without the tremendous presence of horror and its scars on our memory

Without exile

Without Canada and the literature courses at the University of British Columbia

Without that autobiography class where the professor encouraged us to write our own

Without the support of the Canada Council, which let me return home and record testimonies

Without the precious moments I spent conversing with Luis Alberto Acuña, Federico and Mimí Alvarez Rojas, Ana María Careaga, Pedro and Matilde Cerviño, Mirta Clara, Pablo Conti, Nora Cortiñas, Miguel D'Agostino, Daniel Flores, Carlos Groisman, Graciela Jaegger, Matilde Mellibovsky, Jorge Méndez, Ricardo Rotchild, Norberto Szurman, Mario Villani, and others who asked that their names not be published but whose voices are heard in this book

Without that professor who insisted that I enter the manuscript in a literary contest

Without Letras de Oro, which twenty years after the military coup of 1976 awarded me a prize

Without the frequent return visits to Argentina, since 1984, to testify, to search, to ask, to insist

Without my friends' rescuing me at the last minute to meet deadlines set by the North-South Press

xiv   **Acknowledgments**

Without Fanny Seldes and Silvia Bravo's getting me out of all
those jams; Marily Canoso and Marina Kendig's rereading
the very latest versions; Ana Martinez's logistical support

Without Alejandro Kaufman's correcting the galley proofs in the
Spanish version

Without Cora Soroker, who, during one of the Mothers' Thursday marches, gave me the drawing for the original cover

Without the conference where I met Cristina de la Torre, who
could not get the translation of *Una sola muerte numerosa*
out of her head

Without Roberta Culbertson and the shared readings at the Virginia Foundation for the Humanities

Without Janis Breckenridge and her unstinting dedication to
proofreading the English translation

Without Hugh Hazelton, translator and poet, who was given the
difficult task of editing this translation by fate, otherwise
known as the University of Virginia Press

Without the San Diego State University and the possibility of writing this page rather than attending departmental meetings

Without Joan Lindgren, translator of the work of Juan Gelman,
who shared her wisdom and passion for language during the
final stages of the translation

Without the profound presence, at each and every step, of those
who are no longer here

This book would not be this book.
How can I acknowledge all of you? To thank you is not
enough.
You are part of this book; we keep each other company.

Translator's Acknowledgments

For their support the translator wishes to thank Carlos Alonso, M. J. Devaney, and Agnes Moncy. And, of course, Nora Strejilevich, whose collaboration every step of the way was essential.

Mary Berg, Eduardo Cosío, Hugh Hazelton, and Andrés Pacheco made many helpful suggestions along the way.

The encouragement of Alex and Erik Woodhouse, as well as the solace and nurturing provided by Erdmann Waniek, helped greatly to smooth the unavoidable bumps on the road.

A grant from the Howard Foundation and the generosity of Emory University greatly facilitated the translation of this book.

A Note on the Translation

In the process of translation some changes and additions to the original version were introduced with the approval of the author or at her suggestion. Some of the testimonies have been quoted directly from the English version of the document in question, namely, *Never Again (Nunca Más)*, *The Flight*, and *Dossier Secreto*. A glossary of terms has been compiled and precedes the list of sources, which has been expanded.

When they stole my name
I was one   I was hundreds   I was thousands
I was no one.
NN was my face stripped
of gesture   of sight   of voice.

My numbered nakedness walked
in line   without eyes   without I's
with them   alone
my alphabet bled dry
by guttural chains
by moans   citizens of a country
without initials.

Eyelid and blindfold
my horizon
only silence and echo
iron bars and night
only a wall with no mirror
to give a wrinkle
a grimace   a perhaps.

Nothing but dead end.

We shall not permit death to run rampant in Argentina.
—Admiral Emilio Massera, 1976

A certain perverse magic turns the key to the front door. Steps rush in. Three pairs of shoes practice a disjointed stomp on the floor, the clothes, the books, an arm, a hip, an ankle, a hand. My body. I'm the trophy of the day. A hide with hollow head, eyes of glass. The make-believe hunters step on me. *Step on a crack, break your mother's back.*

This ritual exorcises my sins inside their temple: a green Ford Falcon with no license plates speeding through red lights up the wrong side of Corrientes Street. No one bats an eye. It's business as usual.

But it's not every day (or is it?) that the laws of gravity are broken. It's not every day that you open the door and four rooms are ripped apart by a cyclone that shatters the past and yanks the hands off the clock. It's not every day that mirrors crack and costumes unravel. It's not every day that you try to escape and the clock has moved, the door is unhinged, the window stuck, and cornered you cry through minutes that do not tick away. It's not every day that you stumble and fall hands behind your back, trapped in a night that tosses about shreds of daily life. Dizzy you whirl in a vortex of scraps of yesterdays and nows crushed by orders and decrees. You get lost amid chairs overturned, drawers emptied, suitcases torn open, colors blanched out, maps slashed, roads severed. You barely make out the echoes reverberating "You thought you could escape, bitch!" as an enormous mouth devours you. Familiar voices perhaps whisper, "She hasn't done

3

anything, neither has he." But you are here, on this side, in this precarious body: soles tattooed on your skin, boots on your back, a gun at the nape of your neck.

"On your feet!" and you stand up, meek, confused, stunned, defeated, and you shriek, "They're taking me away, they're taking me away!" as claws of steel dig into your flesh. Shoved with impunity into the elevator at two in the afternoon, dragged out of the building, space vanishing under your feet. On the sidewalk you kick and scream against a nameless fate in some mass grave.

I hurl my name with every last fiber—with lungs, with guts, with legs, with arms, with rage. My name flails wildly on the edge of defeat. The animal trainers order me to jump from the high platform into the void. They push me. I land on the floor of a car. Blows rain on me: "Take that for screaming in Jewish, and this for kicking." And this and this.

"You Yid piece of shit, we're gonna make soap out of you." I'm a toy to be broken. *Step on a crack, break your mother's back.*

Keep in mind that I have killed three or four people with my own hands.—Admiral Emilio Massera

> *A, B, C, D,*
> *Let's pray, playmates, agree.*
> *E, F, and G,*
> *Well, so shall it be.*
> *J, K, and L,*
> *In peace we wish to dwell.*

A chorus of voices against a background splotched with brilliant colors. Green, the hedge that separates my house from the neighbors'; white, the garden flagstones on which *the choo-choo train keeps on rollin' and rollin';* red, the courtyard tiles, which sway as I swing; brown, the floor that stretches across the bedrooms. In the kitchen a silver smudge, the kettle; in the bathroom a shimmering surface, the mirror for making faces; in my parents' bedroom the voile curtains, my party dresses; in our room the lamp, a globe round as *The Red Balloon,* a film we saw in school. The red balloon follows the boy everywhere, but mine doesn't know how to fly and just waits for me on the ceiling. It's well-behaved and very pretty, with leaves painted green and a butterfly perched in the middle. I always fall asleep counting the little leaves on my side. My brother has fewer because he doesn't take care of them. Tonight the balloon appears even rounder because our beds have been pushed together. Mama and Papa have gone out, leaving our mattresses side by side: our bed looks really big, just like theirs. We also have permission to watch TV until late if, and only if, we're good.

Gerardo has chosen the program. He always gets his way because I'm younger. He's watching a fight: mounds of tense muscles tearing into each other, blows flying back and forth. I'm scared, and he takes advantage of this to tease me. He stands there making faces: he pulls out his cheek with one hand, pushes up his nose with the other, sticks out his tongue, and leaps to the chase. If I hide under the sheets, he turns out the lights and lunges to devour me. If I try to escape, he blocks the way. I yell, I hit, I push until I break free and run. I run out the front door. I run away to anywhere.

The dark, empty lots don't scare me. I get as far as the cemetery without catching sight of any ghosts. I rush across the street and knock on a door. A pair of arms lifts me up. When I realize what I've just done my legs begin to quiver. The grown-ups fuss over me, and I smile, safe, high up in their arms. I twirl round and round, endlessly, like the butterfly on my globe lamp.

"I fooled you, I fooled you, nani nani boo boo." I left you all alone, and now it's you who's going to be scared to death. You're gonna have an asthma attack. *Good night / Sleep well / Thank you /*

Same to you / You're welcome / Good night. Tonight no one's gonna answer because I get to sleep with them.

Gerardo bothering his little sister, Gerardito lifting her onto his shoulders, Nora upset because he pulls her hair, Norita giggling when he tickles her.

"Shhhush! Be quiet or we'll get a scolding!"

Cat and dog chasing 'round the yard, hiding under the porch, scuffling all over again.

Bring the knife / ring the bell / when you die / you'll go to hell.

Twenty years later, in 1977, the country is different. Our house has changed too. Black, the balcony railing, my mutilated garden; gray, the half-closed shutters, shadows of imaginary trees; brown, the floor that stretches across the apartment; white, the doorframe, our final stage set.

"Look out the window and check to see if I'm being followed," you say, carefully holding the words by the edges to keep them lighthearted.

"What's the use? Here we're living under a dictatorship, and you play hide-and-seek with the bogeyman."

You get angry and leave. I look out to see if they're following you. I see no one. Nor do I see you again.

In order for Argentina to achieve internal security, as many people as necessary will have to die.—General Jorge Rafael Videla, head of the military junta, 10 October 1975

I saw her today at the Plaza Dorrego flea market, among pigeons, tango dancers and accordions, little toy musicians forged out of old forks and spoons, phonographs, antique coins, sheets embroidered by great-great-grandmothers, old stamps, and tourists. Right next to the well covered with small picture frames containing advice for parents, she sits surrounded by her ever-present paper flowers, wearing sandals and a hat adorned with petals in reds, lilacs, yellows, blues, and greens. The spectrum of her many years settled at the very center of this Sunday.

"If you don't tell me they're pretty, you'll have to pay a toll," she chides an audience that, eager for endearments, photographs her as if she were some kind of celebrity. "When I was a teacher, I didn't give a hoot for principals, inspectors, report cards, bells, anything institutional. I was always rebelling against all the silly rules, against the whole system." She flashes her broad smile, rearranges wisps of hair, and adds, "Now I wear a flowered hat and they accept me, even if I'm eccentric, which only goes to show how stupid this society really is."

During geography lessons she never hung up the maps. Instead, she spread them on the floor so the whole class could walk on them. "We went to Europe together, we bundled up for the South Pole, we lay in the Brazilian sun. Those kids got to know the world with me."

Teacher and sweet little old lady. Her flowers, she warns us, are for seducing men. "Just give some to the one you like, sit back, and wait. It never fails."

That's how she got herself a lover, since she's never been married. The only ones who get to hear her story are the privileged few who, like me, arrive at her house without paying the toll. In her bedroom, framed by the curving branches of twining floral arrangements, I spot the picture of her beloved, his aquiline nose under the inevitable military cap. It is the ex-Commander-in-Chief himself, General Jorge Rafael Videla.

"He offered me several positions, but I refused them all. I'm not an opportunist, like those madwomen in the Plaza de Mayo, those *locas* who go around making demands. They want to become famous on account of a few missing agitators. There weren't that many, you know, and besides they were all guerrillas." She has it straight from the horse's mouth, General Videla, whom she loved for twenty-five fleeting and glorious years. "He knew nothing of the murders; he was betrayed by his own men. He told me so himself when I visited him in jail."

I picture them embracing under embroidered sheets, the military cap—as pure and pristine as his ideas—on the night table, the very dawn when Gerardo was plucked from his bed for subversive activities.

HE IS NOT, in essence, a political man. He will very likely carry out his duties in the same style that has characterized his leadership in the Army: a low profile, carefully measured steps, a moderate approach, nothing rash.—*La Opinión*, 19 March 1976

We conduct our operations between one and four in the morning, when the subversives are asleep.—General Acdel Vilas

Gerardo is taking part in a relay race for first graders. The spectators are clapping. On your marks, get set, . . . go!

Gerardito sprints to the front of the pack. Suddenly he stops, turns his head 180 degrees, grins, and waves: Mama is there. He takes off again at top speed but comes in last. He bursts into tears.

Gerardo is in high school but still does not wear long pants. He's a year ahead of his classmates.

Gerardito wants to be an orchestra conductor, but his parents convince him otherwise.

Gerardito is a troublemaker and always gets caught.

Gerardo is smart but slacks off.

Gerardo changes schools after being expelled. He has more demerits than hairs on his head.

Gerardo has knee surgery to avoid the draft.

Gerardo goes to college. He does not have a job.

Gerardo speaks out at political rallies at that damned university.

Gerardito has a girlfriend and sneaks her into the house to spend the night.

Gerardo churns out political fliers on Papa's typewriter. Gerardito is fun, clever, friendly, and a real daredevil.

Gerardo writes too much:

In our country there is an orchestra composed of:

The Great Orchestrator: Mr. Bourgeois.

Conductor: John D. Repressor.

Musicians: field and factory workers, with special appearances by some middle-class players.

The music, composed in Buenos Aires, is divided into three movements:

economic (imperialism vivace)
social (jailhouse andante with molto state of siege)
political (fugue in fraud major)

Gerardo is being watched. He does not sleep at home.

Gerardo supports violence from below and challenges violence from above.

Gerardo lives in fear because he's being followed.

Gerardo reflects:

Suddenly it's clear to you: a flash of awareness that you're not forever. As if they'd casually taken a chunk out of you and then scornfully warned you, "Watch out, kid," hinting that like it or not, slowly but surely, they'd continue chipping away at you until there was nothing left but ashes.

Gerardo almost certainly never killed and certainly never kidnapped anyone.

Gerardo has almost certainly been kidnapped and is almost certainly dead.

I never heard from him again.—Nora Strejilevich, *Nunca Más*

Milicos */ we have no fear / what did you do / with the ones who dis-appeared?*

In 1984 the freshly restored democracy is greeted with waves of chants, slogans, pleas, and demands that flood the streets and pierce the darkness, slicing it into infinite planes of sound.

No mistakes and no excess / you're murderers / all milicos */ in the Process . . .*

Chants fill the void—that concept you could never get me to understand. And now I have nothing to give to you, who so often spoke to me of lines and points in the space-time continuum, not a plane, a vector, a line, not even a grave. I fill the void with voices, which at least distract me from so much blood, with letters that throb to the touch. I can write only vowels and consonants that barely invoke you. Words, only words remain. Your name is bodiless, fleshless, your name is weightless, your name is remorseless—your name.

I spot the corner where marchers are gathering, but before I can take a step you cut in front of me. I bump into your first name, into our last name scrawled across a shameless strip of white cloth. Your black letters sting my memory, and my legs take on a will of their own. I stand there, rooted before your one-dimensional scream.

Bring the knife / ring the bell / when you die / you'll go to hell. My ragged guilt gets entangled in these rhymes.

Tears elude you, hover about you. I need to get a window on this vast truth. I seek a perspective, a frame to hold up my burden. Nothingness is as difficult to grasp as the principle of uncertainty.

Return them alive and punish the guilty . . . Chills run down my spine and I'm unable to join the chorus of voices. Silently, I register the words: *In some woods of northern lands / the weather was icy frost / let's just send the* milicos *out there / and have them all get lost.*

There's a clatter of cymbals and drums. Graciela is at your side, your ethereal girlfriend, who floated to the swaying of her straight hair and tiptoed down the hall of our house in her pajamas. Your strategy for not getting caught, so carefully planned, disintegrated before the family banner of authority. The verdict was swift: banished from the house for a week, exiled for disobedience. In a few hours the sentence was reduced to a mild injunction against bringing her back.

Graciela's block letters are no longer as timid as in those early days. It seems that time—I was going to say life—has made her defiant, even bold. Now the letters are every bit as big as yours. But her last name, voluptuous and graceful, is better than yours at catching the eye: Barroca. It sounds like musical scales, brush strokes, poetry. Like a tragically beautiful destiny. A first-rate last name—her military legacy.

Yours, on the other hand, is thoroughly second-rate: an interminable Jewish name, one of those tongue twisters that drive the locals right up the wall. A mark of difference, in any case, and not of the best kind. It carries with it a pathetic onus exposed by a shift in the wind.

No wonder the members of the antisubversive unit seem so irritated with the former Navy man, Barroca, as they wait for Graciela in the dining room of her house.

"Why on earth did you allow your daughter to get mixed up with a Jew?"

Wrong premise: he had not allowed her. Everything had happened without his consent, much like this forced entry. His words were no longer taken as orders by anyone. He was finished. Even his military sixth sense could not detect that the commando group surrounding his house was not a guerrilla unit.

"Open the door or we'll blow up the house!" They're well

aware that the owner is a minor officer, retired from the Navy. Therefore, with all due respect, they order him to come out, hands up.

We opened the door and asked the men to identify themselves, to no avail. We had no choice but to come out with our hands up. That's when I saw that the windows in the back were smashed. Aside from those initial damages, they had planted explosives along the front of the house and threatened to blow it all up if the family did not comply.

Poodle in arms, hair standing on end, heart skipping. A towel over the parrot's cage so it won't screech. At dusk the prey comes to the front door.

The men were all in civilian clothes. There were eight of them, armed with automatic weapons, hand grenades, and handcuffs. My youngest daughter and I were blindfolded, put in different rooms, and interrogated at length about the habits of the whole family. They were looking for our daughter Graciela and presumed our house was a hideout for terrorists. She had gone to study for a test with a friend and returned home at 10 P.M. At one in the morning, after painstakingly searching the house, the man in charge approached my husband to inform him that they were taking her away for further questioning by a captain. They had found nothing. Still, she did belong to a Peronist student organization, a group founded by a career military man, Juan Domingo Perón himself. So what could they accuse her of?

A swarm of machine guns guides her to the Ford Falcon without license plates. The family is advised not to go to the police with reports that would harm the officer's reputation. In a few days everything will be back to normal. Needless to say, unfortunate accidents do sometimes happen during these operations in totally unpredictable ways and, of course, against the wishes of the personnel involved.

My husband filed a writ of habeas corpus, reported the kidnap-
ping to the police (who informed him that they had explicit orders
from the Army not to intervene), and went to the Ministry of the In-
terior dozens of times until he gave up, feeling that he was just be-
ing strung along.

> CASE 754. It has not been proven conclusively that Graciela
> Barroca was taken from her residence on ——— Street in the
> city of Buenos Aires and stripped of her freedom on 15 July
> 1977.
> There were no eyewitnesses to the event, nor was the
> woman in question seen in any detention center thereafter. All
> we have on the case is the original report, given at the time of
> filing the writ of habeas corpus, but said report remains uncor-
> roborated by any tangible evidence.—*La sentencia*

Your last name, Gerardo, seems to take up more and more
space. An ever-expanding space that cannot be brought to order
without generating entropy, as you would say. I am just now beginning to understand—the military, in their efforts to control
chaos, are only deepening the disorder of the universe. Chaos
control is carried out in accordance with a clearly stated doctrine
and very systematic methods: dissidents are selected and removed from the social fabric. Preventive medicine. It is applied to
me too, and it works.

**That day, 16 July 1977, after searching the whole house and
removing books and papers . . . they took Nora.**—*Nunca Más*

The ride from my neighborhood to the death camp, the so-called
Athletic Club, takes about fifteen minutes on Saturdays, when
there's little traffic. The distance gets covered in a flash because
the driver, a veteran champion of kidnap joyrides, floors it to 100
mph. When the tires roll over dirt, I realize we're here, in the
only existing glacial circle of hell.

"The kid misbehaved, did she? Uh-oh, looks like we'll have to give her a little spanking. Strip naked, bitch!"

It all happens so fast that I don't remember how or where I get out of my clothes, even though I'm not in the habit of undressing in public. I do it on my own in a split second, but I still get berated by their rifle butts.

There is one advantage to not being able to see. I can ignore their presence. That is, unless they talk to me. And these guys talk. Or rather, they bark orders.

"Lie on your back." It's a cold metal table. They tie me down.

Men quick to unzip

The four armed men don't tie me up as they shove me into the car. Since I'm pregnant when they come for me, I think I'm being taken to a hospital, to a maternity ward for detainees. But the men are wearing civilian clothes, and when I ask them to identify themselves, they simply mumble. They drive right past the turn-off to the hospital and keep on going until they reach a crossroads. There I see a patrol wagon and several police cars. They make me get in the truck, which is filled with prisoners who are being transferred. I realize that I'm without any kind of legal protection.

The trip seems endless, although it is probably quite short. Time can unravel in your own hands, as Cortázar says. We're so packed in there that, being eight and a half months pregnant, I begin to break down. The prisoners bang on the sides of the van, and the policemen stop. When they come around to the back I'm told, "Actually, we've no idea who you are."

How do you live among people who have no idea who you are, in blind alleys that don't show on any maps? Among men who, without a qualm, earn their daily bread by asking how you like it—from the front or from the rear? Men quick to unzip who open and close their flies with masterful swiftness, the result of extensive training. A very masculine way of subduing the enemy.

I am crucified, hands and feet tied to an icy table. They are ready for action. "C'mon whore, let's hear it." How, when, where was my first time.

> WHEN THEY KIDNAPPED that girl, they asked her which torture she preferred—the cattle prod or rape.
> At first she chose the prod, but then she asked to be raped. The next day one of the guards inquired:
> "What did they do to you last night?"
> "They raped me, sir."
> "Bitch, [*slaps*] no one did anything to you here, understand?"
> "Yes, sir."
> "What happened to you last night?"
> "Nothing, sir."—Ana María Careaga, *Nunca Más*

"Don't you remember anything? Was it standing up or lying down? From the front or from the rear? Did your parents find out?" they ask over and over.

They said to me, "Hey, you wouldn't want your husband to find out about this." I was thinking, yes, he's surely bound to hear. But no, he never heard a thing. They gagged me and threw me down on my own bed. I wanted to scream but couldn't. I thought, I hope I die.

Death is the only way out, I kept telling myself. They have all the time in the world, and you feel that dying is the only way to stop the endless suffering.

And the voices continue, relentless in their curiosity: "When was it, day or night?"

It happened in broad daylight. Coming home from school I get into the elevator with a stranger. He's fat and traps me between his belly and the mirror. "How old are you?" he whispers through clenched teeth, while rubbing his flab against my body.

A hand gropes eagerly among the pleats of my smock, fondling, pinching, cornering me. I smell something blue. A glove covers my mouth. A voice promises pleasures I don't understand. When we reach the third floor I push past him, burst out the door, and run away. The blue smell stays there.

I break free from one prison only to be confined to another. I'm afraid to go out and afraid to stay home, afraid to move, afraid to feel afraid. Tomorrow he'll be there, at school. Tomorrow must not come. I take refuge in the present moment, inside the walls of our apartment, spying on the ominous rhythms of the street. Girls, young women, mothers strolling alone on sidewalks. Something is sure to happen to them as they turn the corner, and then their windows will grow metal grilles.

My obsession won't let up. Endless days, months. An endless year of observing bodies tread down the street, each with its heavy sexual cargo. I walk to school holding Papa's hand. I play at undressing the teacher and find her pathetic, with gray-sprinkled pubic hair and sagging breasts. During history class I envision armies of rapists, in geography I imagine continents of flesh, mountains of fat like that belly.

I'm not sure whether it was exhaustion, boredom, or weakness that finally drove me out of the house and into the streets again, hand in hand with my first love. I got over the nightmares of a solitary winter and summer. Suddenly there were two of us, my body a new territory with each caress. Language blossomed with words new to my senses. I was a woman, and so I desired.

Our passion, Gabriel, is a rapture barely restrained by my shyness, a blend of poetry written in lined notebooks, of eyes closed or half-turned, of mouths whispering tomorrows. I'm your muse, and I accept your gifts under the autumn drizzle as peace offerings after our quarrels. Reconciliations are sealed with a kiss, and the search for the sunset ends in duets along train tracks leading to La Boca, your barrio. La Boca for walks, La Boca for laughs, La Boca to be with you. You compose music for me, while I only manage to write you a letter. I don't know how or why the spell is broken, but one day you embrace me and you're different. Or I am. I no longer want to be anyone's muse. I borrow words to say good-bye.

Good-bye cruel world

Good-bye session. They drag me to a cell to think it over. The guard is now a soft voice, intimate, paternal: "Calm down, sweetheart, relax." A voice that walks away singing *Good-bye cruel world / I'm leaving you today / Good-bye / good-bye / good-bye / good-bye all you people / there's nothing you can say.*

If I still had a roof in my mouth, if I had a tongue, or lips, I might smile. No, I couldn't. My body is possessed by a death rattle.

"You're a piece of shit, you don't exist," another voice adds. There's only pain. The unreality of the world settles in somewhere between my gums and my molars. Beyond that, nothing.

> ELECTRODES ON YOUR TEETH . . . each hideous bolt of thunder cracking your head open . . . a thin cord with tiny little balls . . . each ball was an electrode, and when they were switched on it seemed as if glass shattered, a thousand pieces spraying your insides, exploding shards that ripped right through you. . . . You couldn't shout, or moan, or move, only shake, a convulsive shaking that, if you hadn't been tied down, would have sent you into fetal position.—CONADEP

I'm shaking, my teeth chatter, everything hurts. I want to see where I am. I pull down the blindfold, and for the first time I open my eyes. It's no use. There's only darkness. This room is like a closet, with barely room to sit. I'm here to think it over. My mind is blank. I can't even think about death. Between my thoughts and me, this compact metal door. They want me to think it over. I can't come up with anything. I'm all out of words. Names, names, and more names. And background music for the jailer's tune: a swarm of cries that are shouts, shouts that are screams, screams that are wails, a volcano of anguish comparable to nothing. Nothing to say, nothing to add. A searing pain like a stitch deep in the thickness of the muscles, in my womb, in my bones. If my body does not fall to pieces, it's only because it's pierced by countless needles. Music. Shocks. And music to muffle the shocks. An impeccable counterpoint.

> NORA STREJILEVICH (file no. 2535) was just finishing packing for a trip to Israel, when a group of people entered her home.—*Nunca Más*

A counterpoint of laments writhes in the distance. Chants in a mysterious tongue, the accompaniment for our Saturdays, waft through the kitchen that faces the temple. I never set foot in the synagogue; it's enough to inhabit this music box to whose rhythms I fold my clothes. The music of cries, silent, silenced, sentenced.

"What were you shouting in Jewish in the street?"

"My last name."

"Pretty soon you won't feel much like playing games with us, you little kike."

> JEWS WERE TAKEN out on a daily basis to be shoved around, beaten up. One day Hitler's speeches were played and they were forced to raise their arms in salute and say, "I LOVE HITLER, HEIL, HEIL, HEIL FUHRER." The guards got a big kick out of this. Then they stripped the prisoners down and spray-painted black swastikas on their bodies.—CONADEP

They tie my hands and feet. Crucified. There's no way around it. I hurt, leave me alone. I'm a stopwatch, a human one perhaps.

"Even if you don't know a thing, you're going to pay just for being a Jew."

THEY THREATENED [Nora] for saying Jewish words in public [her last name] and for being a hymie shit, said she was good for soap.—CONADEP

THEY CENTERED the interrogation around Jewish matters. One of them could speak Hebrew, or at least a few words, which he could place in the correct order in a sentence. He tried to find out if there was any military training in the kibbutzim. They asked for a physical description of the organizers of the study tours, like the one I was on (Sherut Laam), a description of the building of the Jewish Agency (which they knew very well), and so on. They assured me that they were primarily concerned with "the problem of subversion," but the "Jewish problem" was next in importance, and they were gathering information for their files.—*Nunca Más*

They know perfectly well every nook and cranny of the building that houses the Jewish Agency. One of them refreshes my memory: "The staircase is at the front, the office where they help the public, upstairs. Remember now?"

Since I refuse to remember the person who helped me there, they describe him in minute detail. Who is this man who knows so much? And if he knows so much, why does he keep asking?

IN THE UNDERGROUND jails where he worked, Julián the Turk paraded around, swinging a key chain with a swastika on it. He was particularly vicious to Jewish detainees, even bringing Nazi propaganda for them to read.—*La Nación*, 2 May 1995

"You're Jewish, but you're all right," the neighbor across the street once told Mama. They were Germans and, according to my parents, SS who had escaped to South America after World War II. My grandparents, on the other hand, are Russians and Poles who arrive in Argentina in 1910, a year of hyperbole—peace, union, and integration. It is the centennial of Argentine independence from Spain, a year bloated with commemorative acts and patriotic anthems. The faith in the country's predestination to greatness is unshakable, the racial melting pot, a fact.

Thousands of eyes look toward America from the steppes and the mountains of eastern Europe. Thousands put their ears to the promising golden ground of the pampas. Upon a landscape of pogroms, migrations, and destruction they project a bucolic vision that requires only their labor. Many come. They dock in Buenos Aires. On its muddy beaches they unload trunks and bundles and strap them onto carts, twenty or fifty years of life wrapped in clothes, memories, menorahs.

"Did you sway with the waves for sixty days and sixty nights? Did you end up lodging in the Immigrants' Hotel with your shipmates? Or did you, that very night, go up the Uruguay River to Entre Ríos?"

Only there do they realize the true dimensions of their task: to become godlike. To make crops sprout without tools, to live without roofs. Or almost. There are some canvas tents, and the untamed horizon is wide-open pastureland. Who knows what stories are woven there. Warmed by the sun and by new rituals, they build ovens, dig wells and ditches, till, keep their plows in good repair, and watch the wheat grow like a vast green sheet. There isn't much—a few rakes and shovels—but many hands learning the soil. Desolation lies hidden behind theater curtains, feasts, prayers, and romantic melodies from remote countries, all of which does little to lessen droughts, locusts, frosts, and floods. Grandfather Isidoro isn't thrilled by country life, or theatrical effects, or plagues. He keeps to himself, then moves to the capital. "Room for Rent" signs are all over Buenos Aires.

Men of few words

In the Buenos Aires of 1977 there is no place to hide. There are no rooms for young activists to rent. It's everyone for himself. And even Gerardo's workplace doesn't offer safety. Several scientists have been kidnapped, yet the director doesn't feel the slightest need to report it. He's a senior admiral, and senior admirals are men of few words.

> BETWEEN October 1976 and September 1978 fourteen physicists, engineers, and other employees of Argentina's continent-leading atomic energy commission were "disappeared" by the security forces.—Andersen, *Dossier Secreto*

The parents met regularly, and I was often asked my thoughts on the fate of our children. Since they were all scientists, some of the parents imagined they might be working in labs or something, down in Patagonia. I was in a real quandary since I couldn't bring myself to lie and I couldn't get up the nerve to say what I truly believed: that there was no such thing as a secret research center.

Gerardo, an atom in the exodus of militants into the underground.

Isidoro, an atom in the exodus of immigrants to the big city. You settled into a place in barrio Once, in the same building that your grandchildren still occupy sixty years later. Did you hang your mattresses on balcony railings to air them out? Did you eat bagels, challah, rugalach? Did you speak Yiddish, that sweet language baked in music? Or was it Yiddish seasoned with a bit of local flavoring? Who knows. One fine day all of you die, and your aspirated *h*'s and sharp *j*'s are buried under headstones carved in Hebrew that I've never seen.

Grandpa, is it true that you peddle cloth from a cart? Do you really travel all the way to Paraguay and push deep into the wild forests to barter with the Indians? What do you get in exchange for those vibrant, brightly colored fabrics? They say that you earn lots of money but that it comes in one hand and goes out the other, that you start up and close down businesses on a whim. Do you lack patience, or are there too many swindlers?

Family members also suffer the consequences of your swings of fortune. They move from tenements into mansions and back again, shedding party clothes for overalls. Papa and José, the oldest, go to the markets to sell religious keepsakes until a stroke of luck sends them back to private school, the Cangallo Schule. That's just where one of the Argentine generals discovered his military calling! And where Papa decided never to speak German again after the war. He just stopped, even though he could recite Goethe by heart.

"A German school? Didn't you go to Jewish schools?"

"No, dear. Your grandparents left those traditions on the boat." They barely kept the custom of tearing their clothes at the passing of a loved one, lighting Shabbat candles, fasting and using brand-new dishes on Yom Kippur. Everything else was forgotten, like the samovar and the sugar cube in the mouth at teatime. Here they drank *mate* and even ate ham. The secret of assimilating into the new culture was to never look back. Doing so would risk divine retribution, as with Lot's wife. Pilgrims to the future, their goal was to give birth to Argentine blood. In America religion didn't matter. What mattered was giving the children a good secular education based on the twin pillars of justice and freedom. God could be forgotten, but not the fact that we had once been slaves in Egypt.

These were the raw materials for a new crop of professionals—doctors, architects, lawyers, and intellectuals who retained but a faint memory of their origins. For the grandchildren it was only a remote echo and a few sepia-colored photographs of bearded old men wearing bowler hats and black capes, or stocky women in long dresses and plaited hair, with a distant look in their eyes.

We, the grandchildren, barely knew what it meant to be Jewish. Was it a religion? A way of life? A race? An identity?

Being a Jew means, simply, being seen as one. But we didn't know this then.

> THEY [those at the Athletic Club] repeatedly asked if he had any Jewish friends. They wanted information, any and all—even the smallest details—about any Jewish merchants or just anyone of that religion with whom he'd had problems.—CONADEP

I can't make out whether what I hear is whispers, a voice questioning me in Sanskrit, or music composed solely in order to confuse, nauseate, revolt, an atonal concert with nonsensical lyrics and spasmodic, strident rhythms. The voice is accompanied by a strange percussion that jolts my skin. It's not blows but rather something that brushes past without stinging or burning or shaking or hurting or drilling but still burns, drills, stings, hurts, shakes. It kills. That humming, that agony, the precarious fraction of a second that precedes the shocks, the loathing for that sharp tip that explodes on contact with the skin, vibrating and hurting and cutting and piercing and destroying brain, teeth, gums, ears, breasts, eyelids, ovaries, nails, the soles of the feet. My head, my ears, my teeth, my vagina, my scalp, the pores of my skin give off a burnt smell.

Half-turn: "Let's see, how about a little shock up the ass?" and they all laugh.

"You understand now that you're dead the moment you get here? Come on, sing!"

My code name, the Trotskyites, my friends, the Montoneros, my brother, my cousins, my neighbor—the names of all of them and more, many more. White light, scorched mouth, shivers. Tendons, muscles, blood all roar guttural words, consonants and vowels. I plead to lower the voltage of the next shock, the voltage of fear. They want names, have to make them up—my brain does not answer.

"I'm a son of a bitch! They pay me to torture and be a son of a bitch!" I will not give these gentlemen the pleasure of my crying. What's the use? Tears do not open locks, my grandmother used to say.

Once I heard someone sobbing. One of them, known as Kung Fu, came and took her out of her cell, led her to the torture chamber, and we could hear her wailing as she was worked over. When they brought her back to her cell we heard them ask, "Are you going to keep on crying?" and she answered, "No, sir."

Tears do not open locks

"Don't cry."

"If I don't cry, will I be like you?"

I want to be just like you, a willful and clever independent woman, to live on my own terms, to have adventures. And I don't want to marry if marriage is the sort of shipwreck you'd rather not talk about.

Your story is frayed at the edges. All that remains is a fable patched together from your tales and my memories, from your fantasies and my dreams.

It is Warsaw, about 1900. The eldest daughter of a large family takes over her father's business. The old man, worn out by so many years of overseeing the fruit pickers, delegates all responsibilities.

Small, lively, two blond braids framing her Slavic face, Kaila sets out for the mountains and steppes to oversee the fields and find new markets. Accustomed to life in the open, to journeys through the snow, to the motion of ships, trains, carts, and horses, she's a stranger to the confines of city life.

One day, back after a long absence, she discovers that in the warmth of her own home her fate lies frozen. She must marry. She refuses. She attempts to rebel: she cries for three days and three nights, but her father will not tolerate a spinster daughter. She's locked up in the little back room to think it over. Since tears do not open locks, she must endure the prison walls. Every day suitors come and go asking for her hand, drawn not so much by the dowry as by the beauty of this woman with stormy ocean-blue eyes, cheekbones like dunes, lips like flower buds. Her resentment deepens. All are rejected. The headstrong maiden, soon to turn thirty, is amused by a handsome youth of about eighteen who knocks on her door. He too is rejected like all the rest, but she's not able to conceal a certain surprise. Several hours later a rumor finds its way to her: the lad is threatening suicide if she does not agree to marry him. My grandmother has no intention of giving in to a spoiled brat, but her father issues an ultimatum:

"You'll be banished from this house if you don't take him as your husband."

Left without options, with not one single voice raised in her support, worn down by threats, by so many locked doors, she relents. She says yes to the lad, no to herself. From then on, she never stops longing for the lost paradise of her freedom. It is her husband who does the traveling now. He decides to cross the ocean in search of the treasures hidden in America.

A second daughter is born as Mauricio is about to leave for Argentina. Once he settles in Buenos Aires, the doors of exile open for all three females. Instead of bundles like before, Kaila carries crying girls who bicker constantly and make an already hateful journey unbearable.

girl is forced to marry

Paradoxically, the only ones to enjoy the New World will be the women. Mauricio dies shortly afterwards, leaving his wife to do the mourning, manage the trade, and feed three daughters. The worst part of the inheritance is the business, since Mauricio, a staunch macho, had kept Kaila in the dark about day-to-day details. Feeling helpless, disoriented, ignorant of local laws and language, she opts to sell and is cheated. With what little she gets, she opens a delicatessen and runs it with the help of her older daughters. The youngest one is able to go to school. As soon as the older ones marry, she closes the shop and withdraws to her home in the back, surrounded by begonias and memories. At last she is free to relive her chosen reality—those thirty years in her native Poland.

I watch her kneading the past in the narrow wood kitchen that looks out onto the lonely patio. That's where we sit, where she tells me stories. I look at her between bites of gefilte fish, between gulps of farfel soup, feeling the brush of her nostalgia in the way she slowly sways while kneading, in her half-closed eyelids, in her plaintive voice:

"If I'd only known, I would never have come."

That sentence

For years you grumble plaintively about being sentenced to married life, Mama, disguising your despondency with songs, melodies, and tunes. You wash, iron, and cook while intoning lyrics that clash with your concise, meticulous style.

What does it matter knowing who I am / where I come from / where I'll end up runs into *Alone, worn out and gaunt / I saw her at dawn leaving the club* in a medley that closes with *Kiss me once more / think that perhaps / we'll never see each other again.* That is, if you're in a good mood. If not, you prefer *Today, it seems, straight or crooked is the same / . . . ignorant, wise, or thieving man / charlatan or good-hearted man . . . / It's all the same! / There's nothing better! / A jackass or a great professor, it's all the same. / The world always has been and will be a filthy mess / that much I know by now / back in 506 and in 2000 too,* and your face burns with rage when you conclude *Twentieth-century bazaar / feverish and foolish mess / if you don't cry, you won't eat / and if you work you're a jerk . . .*

This tango was, for good reasons, forbidden by the military leaders when they grabbed *the frying pan by the handle / and made off with the dough.*

Perhaps singing out loud, in your clear lilting voice, is a way to put some shine on your homely routine, your life in a gilded cage. Papa tries to amuse you with comments that he pulls out of his pockets while pacing up and down the corridor.

But you're no longer amused. True, you were not a victim of the slave trade between Warsaw and Buenos Aires. But you certainly did not travel first class on your way to a life altogether lacking in drama. A past in the brothels would have sparked the imagination much better than the sensible series of events that you summarily recount as your story. Saleslady in a hat shop, courted one New Year's Eve, married to only one husband, mother of two children. Your life is an irrelevant broken record, a wax one at that, outdated and with no value other than that granted by a few layers of time.

Fortunately, there are some people who don't resemble their lives. As soon as you take the stage, one begins to doubt your biography. You have a stately presence, an aristocratic look that doesn't go with the apron and the rubber gloves. Lithe, with fine features and delicate fingers—an altogether classy ensemble. The jarring clash of character and costume is exacerbated as soon as you speak, for your opinions raise eyebrows. You are on occasion daring, often impetuous, always vehement. You're used to being heard, obeyed. Not only do you exercise rigorous control over each and every corner of the family space, but your mind is populated by exotic characters and delicious anecdotes that you entertain us with at snack time—about going with grandfather to the circus, where they staged scenes from an Argentine version of *The Thousand and One Nights,* with Scheherazade dressed in oriental garb and brewing *mate;* about the house that Uncle David built after winning the lottery, with two floors exactly alike, one to live in and the other for spare, covered in newspapers to keep it clean; about the misadventures of Samuel, that wicked doll with the huge ears and deep pasty voice, collector of dilapidated cars for use as makeshift beds in five or six service stations scattered around the city. In one of them you must have parked your fantasy that July of 1977.

> FUCKING SCUM, how dare they provoke us right here, under our very nose, and we even let them. They're nothing but a bunch of communists, mothers of subversives, and still they have the nerve to march and make demands. If only they'd let me, I'd sweep the Plaza clean with machine-gun fire. I can guarantee they wouldn't be back.—A military officer

Nowadays you make your way alone, Mama, to a plaza surrounded by flower beds with a monument in the middle. Every Thursday you go, at once shy and defiant, to walk in circles, arms linked with other women, wearing a similar white kerchief on your head, the same absence in a photo, an absence that keeps you walking round and round. Walking, walking, and finding out so many things as you walk.

For me the Plaza is where we meet with our children. Entering the circling crowd is a sacred act, a ritual that each one experiences in her own private way. There are times when one has to remain silent and not listen to the persons nearby: it's the moment for remembering. On the other hand, every Thursday you run into someone you hadn't seen there before, and your embrace vibrates with memories. There is a flow of emotions in the mothers' encounter that is unlike the usual, everyday kind. The Plaza, above all, is the strongest site of indictment there is: the demonstrations upset the church, upset the politicians, and even some of the passersby, who mutter, "These old hags are still here."

Right next to the same old hags, the same old boots belonging to the same old guards. "Keep moving, keep moving," and you acquiesce in your own way and do keep moving, a circle of mothers and children holding hands.

They put up fences to keep us out, but we always went back, despite the police harassment. We all tried to be booked for disorderly conduct. Two, five, sometimes twenty mothers would be taken to the police station, and the rest stayed on the street, all through the night, taking turns. The mothers were usually kept in jail a few days and then released.

Once, when we got to the Plaza, we saw that the whole mounted police unit was there. I had to pass between two rearing horses, because they purposefully pricked them to make them jittery. I was really scared. Another time they chased us, and we ran to take shelter in the cathedral. When the priests saw us coming, they closed the doors. "Don't you have mothers?" we shouted at them. Hebe, our leader, always remembers how they came to clear us out of the Plaza with machine guns loaded for battle and how they even got to the point of shouting "AIM!" and we countered by yelling "FIRE!"

"Fire!"
"I'm not dead! I'm not dead!"—Federico García Lorca, before being executed

"You're going to kill me! Stop! You're kiiiilling meeee!"

Gerardo? It's him. It's Gerardo's voice. That certainty paralyzes me, gives me vertigo, but I don't have time not to react.

"I don't know anything! Stop!"

His moans rip me apart, tear me into countless shreds. It's him, he must be in a room nearby, or could it be a recording to make me speak? They keep drilling into me, the voltage feels higher than ever, I bite my tongue to keep from exploding.

"Look, man, the same scar as on that other guy, just like a factory label!" It's the marks on our backs from infected vaccinations, signs of our identity that we both wear like badges. They have you. Yes, you are here.

"Stop! You're kiiiilling meeee!"

And they're killing you! No, don't pierce me with that scream! Don't let them kill you! My voice breaks as it fleetingly joins yours. Then there is silence. I no longer hear you. I no longer feel myself.

DURING THE interrogation session I could hear the screams of my brother and his girlfriend, whose voices I could make out perfectly. In addition, the torturers referred to a scar that both of us—my brother and I—have on our backs, which confirmed his presence there.—Nora Strejilevich, *Nunca Más*

They want me to confess. Now that I know Gerardo is here, it's less likely than ever. And besides, confess to what?

"If you don't talk, it's your death warrant. If you don't talk, you're dead."

The phrase echoes dryly, floating on the stench of their breath. My life hangs from the thread of that clear and distinct notion. Death as a deadline, a form to be filled out on time. A warrant—a single sheet of letterhead stationery, a notice that will never even make it into the newspapers. It will barely even reach the hands of the men who mastermind the operations.

THE MASTERMINDS were there, the ones who made the decisions. They didn't mix with the prisoners. Making contact with

the reality of freeing or killing a person is a cruel thing . . . none of them wanted to have anything to do with the prisoners.
—Julián the Turk, *Crónica*, 4 May 1995

Making contact with reality through the newspaper is like reading a horoscope: the predictions can be interpreted so many different ways. Mama reads aloud: "High-ranking officials promise that after a thorough study of the issue of the disappeared, a well-considered answer will be given." As he listens, Papa sips a *mate* in order to keep his tongue still.

"Any more details?"

"No, be patient."

"Be patient!" they told us. "We cannot provide instant solutions. You'll get an answer soon. Come back tomorrow."

The plan was being carried out to perfection: courteous treatment, nothing so concrete that it might offer any hope, pretending to look into matters, to care, in order to string people along. It dawned on me that nothing I could do as an individual would have any effect, and so I joined the Mothers. It was no longer a question of finding just your own child, but each and every one of the missing children. Motherhood became a collective enterprise.

What pamphlets?

"Why all these socialist books? What kind of pamphlets were you printing at home? Who were you living with in El Tigre? Talk!"

Talk about Roberto and his crazy ways? About his habit of shopping the sales for useless gadgets? About his suddenly pawning the furniture to pay off unexpected debts? About the inventions he was going to sell to unknown African countries? The last straw: his own printing press.

There's no way to stop that monster once it's cranked up, a beastly machine. I curse the day you brought it home. It prints page after page while spewing green ink that splatters all over, making us roar with laughter. Its tantrums, those unpredictable spots, ruin hours of work. Hours of writing, editing, printing, putting together an impossible *Review of Philosophy*, which we distribute and even buy up when clients are scarce.

The term *client* is not gratuitous. Not readers, clients. Roberto adopts a very businesslike tone. The game starts out from one shore, irony, and slowly makes its way across to the other, good deals in many styles. You swim between humor and retail sales but sink at the moment of truth.

Buenos Aires, 21 October 1974

Dear Nora,

I'm obliged to inform you that as payment for last night's movie tickets our firm requires the following services:

Quotes from Marx and Hegel	4
Caresses	9
Smiles	16
Kisses	3
Total	32

Please remit payment at your earliest convenience.

The signature is that of a stranger, the sales manager, who includes a return address. I answer in the same tone and casually add my phone number. For a whole year we play at dating. You dial my number, I wait for your calls from every direction on the compass. From El Tigre, from downtown, from all your regular haunts—your job at the newspaper, your parents' house, the university, bars, and a fifth location constantly shifting in Brownian motion. In order not to lose each other in so many possible misencounters, we opt for living under one roof. Thus all come into being—our swarm of dreams, crossings and separations, communications, and endless short circuits.

Our apartment grows around us, and we become a couple.

The parrot green walls of the early days are whitewashed and rooms are born; legs sprout from cardboard boxes and we have chairs; metal roads cut through mountains of books and the library is born; the mattress becomes a bed; soon there's a refrigerator and the habit of eating at home; easy chairs, and the habit of stretching out to read. My paintings and your maps, our whims and quirks, daily life. When our days pulsate almost in synch, our nights begin to suffer from arrhythmia. Infrequent caresses make our hearts beat at different speeds. Night separates us, making us distinct and naked beings even as day sews us back together with invisible stitches. Gradually the nights grow longer, as in winter, and paint the walls black. Our cozy happiness ebbs away in easy monthly installments. You sell the record player, and the music that accompanied our silences ends; gone too are the table, the nightstand, the curtains, the mirror. The house becomes a stranger, just like us. On the day we pack up, the remains of our precarious romance fit into two meager suitcases.

We split up without those stacks of papers that pile up after a divorce. The doorman can finally have his say. Fed up with mumbling "señor" and "señora" greetings when he knows full well—I'm not sure how—that we're not married, he daringly and casually uses the word *señorita* as I'm walking out of the building. He says it pointedly, looking directly at me, his mouth curled up into a knot. The high moral ground on which he stands puts a flush on his cheeks.

"Good-bye, señorita."

Tradition condemns me from the lofty heights of the righteous. A man who hastens to fulfill his civic duty by alerting security forces about two suspicious young adults who have just vacated their dwelling, leaving behind a printing press, in all likelihood used for subversive purposes. They break into the apartment.

How could we ever have moved into a neighborhood that was crawling with Army people? How could we not have sensed the suspicion seeping out of every window? In the Argentina of 1977 every young person was guilty until proven innocent. We overlooked that basic premise, and we lost.

After a safe interval, Roberto attempts to rescue whatever's left. From the bridge he makes out the usual landscape: children playing on the grass under yellow lime trees. He walks up to the fourth floor. The place has been totally ransacked: doors kicked in, lights on, furniture upside down, floors ripped up, mountains of torn-up books, paintings, maps, broken chairs. The Beatles records are black splinters stuck onto a grim musical score.

They threw the records on the floor and stepped all over them. The only thing they had against that boy was that he'd gotten a scholarship to a "dangerous" country. Before taking their leave they broke down the door.

Human beings can also break down. Not quite like glass, but almost. Shards of glass can be thrown out, but human debris gets recycled into men and women with a brand-new identity. This sometimes happens in the netherworld of the disappeared, the result of treatments applied in centers for redesigning humans. The resurrected still have the same fingerprints, but they've been fitted with a brand-new odometer that reads zero miles and a motor that speeds along sweeping away everything in its path. It's not clear how or when someone might experience such a breakdown. What is known, though, is the aftereffects: now these persons swim in the banality of evil like fish in the water, and if there are guilt feelings, they simply wait them out. Every prisoner worries about breaking down. How long will I be able to take it? Is it worth it to resist when others are talking? Escaping from yourself, however, is not that simple. So I pledge to be true to myself, always. I will not turn away from myself for anything. I will walk with my shadow even if I cannot see it. I succeed thanks to a technique that obliterates memory. Memory must coagulate and take on a life apart, far from here, among its own characters and landscapes.

Remember nothing

I don't remember the number of my cell, the prisoner number I wore in jail, or what the cell itself was like. The only thing I do recall is a window, but not whether the beds were of metal or wood. I remember the toilet of Sierra Chica and how that prison felt like a vault. I remember the so-called donkey, a kind of storage closet, and not much more. I don't remember the uniform, except that it was gray and blue, but I do remember a spider and a line of verse that said "loneliness falls from the ceiling like an immense spider." I remember very little else.

The strategy is to remember nothing. I don't remember the faces or the meetings, or the smoke, or the excitement, or the passwords, or the clapping, or the friends, or the lovers, or the neighbors.

The urgency to forget situations, to forget partners, to forget faces was such that I really did forget them. For nothing, right? Because finally, after being locked up for half a year, one of the milicos came and told me that I'd be freed the next day. It was there that I learned to hate their omnipotence, because I experienced it directly. That last day in prison I found out what I'd been accused of. I was charged with being a Montonero; they stated that subversive material had been found under my mattress. I told them that I'd have to be a total idiot to keep such compromising stuff under my mattress when there were plenty of hills in which to bury something like that. The guy thought for about three minutes and then said, "Yeah, I guess you're right. Tomorrow you'll be set free." He wrote down my name and left.

Names, na-mes, naaaaaames, n-a-m-e-s. The names of my classmates, my brother's friends, my cousin's wife, the ones traveling to Israel with me, or rather, without me. Names: John Doe, Joe Blow, so and so. I don't know what to invent to avoid contradicting myself. Fortunately my memory is very poor and I can hardly remember anyone. For instance, I don't remember wicked Patricia, my twin, my double.

Yes, my double

For years we unwittingly followed in each other's footsteps. When you walked into the theater of shadows, I'd just left; when I started taking music lessons, you were already finished. You knew Gerardo, I knew your boyfriend, but our paths never crossed. We were the same age, the same height, looked vaguely alike, and followed the same unmarked routes that finally came together.

A waiting room, two chairs facing each other. They're interviewing for a trip, that stealthy escape hatch from the armed camp that our country had become by 1977. The military is not really interested in us, but the air is unbreathable, fouled by sinister rumors. That two blocks up the street they took away a whole family, including a baby; that they came back for the TV and the furniture in broad daylight; that one of the perpetrators was seen; that they cordoned off the street; that screams were heard; that the landlord too was taken.

Buenos Aires, 16 July 1977. The day we're supposed to leave from Ezeiza Airport. You search everywhere: the airline counter, the gate, the shops, the restrooms, the halls, the telephones, the main lobby area. You have me paged over the public-address system. Nothing. What a maddening talent for lateness, you wail in panic rather than rage. When the plane takes off, everything splits in two. I do not show up, you leave. You soar, I sink; you're in the air, I'm earthbound; wings for you, terror for me. The plane carries off my dreams, packed away in your luggage; I'm still free to mock the simplistic logic of guns. I go with you even if I didn't keep our appointment. In fact, I must confess that I forgot all about it. But in the country of "I don't remember," I think secretly about you—you can't imagine just how much. Enough to say that when you land in Israel you are my double. Yes, my double, with an almost impossible mission: taking charge of my dreams without abandoning yours. The idea is born when they leave me alone, through days that are nights and nights that are also nights. That infinite sameness is pierced by a theater of shadows, and I realize that I knew you before. Darkness helps me envision your childhood with stunning clarity. I see you inventing people in another basement, frowning impatiently because your characters are reluctant to be born and spring into existence. You're eager to wake them, until finally Gilgamesh appears with his lament in the city of Ur. The first lament of a man for another's death, that of his friend Enkidu. The rage at his loss echoes all the way from Mesopotamia; from behind the black cardboard masks comes a breath of life four thousand years old. Peering into castles and over hills, you smile in musical scores that move to the sound of your own imaginary key.

Come help me fight off death with your rage, Patricia. It's time to put into practice what we learned behind the scenes. I'm the shadow, you're the hand. Since you are my double, nothing of mine is foreign to you. You will divine my shadowy dreams, enabling me to leave my cave and stand in the sun there, in Jerusalem.

Moths

They have my book *Oh Jerusalem!* They read me whole paragraphs from it. Not so much to demonstrate that they can read as
to delve into my relations with Irgun terrorists.

"But the Irgun split up in 1948!"

That seems to pacify them—and they'd be even calmer if they
only knew that the Irgun was not a leftist group—but new questions emerge:

"How come you had Marx in your library? What else were
you reading? Talk!"

> THE CAMPAIGN against books was carried out by the Army it-
> self. They did the rounds of downtown bookstores, pulling
> books off shelves and tables. I remember one of those episodes,
> witnessed by hundreds of people, a few days after the Videla
> coup. It was a huge bookstore lined with tables piled high with
> books old and new. A military truck stopped right in front, and
> the macabre ritual began. . . . Books hit the floor with a thud.
> People remained silent. Just like kidnapped children, those
> books had no voice with which to speak in their own
> defense. . . . The "purge" of the books was a so-called "intelli-
> gence" operation. An army that burns books can never win a
> war.—Bayer, *Rebeldía y esperanza*

I love to open and close huge illustrated books with hard,
bright red covers. Open: a wolf peeks out from between the
pages disguised as a little old grandmother. Close: the traveling
ant walks away, her wooden shoes leaving footprints on the dusty
path. Books are my playhouses. I am director, spectator, even
protagonist. Whatever I please.

One day, standing on tiptoe, I reach the grown-ups' shelf. I
pull out thick volumes with lots and lots of letters. *Black Beauty* is
my favorite. A wild, jet-black horse remembers his first home on

a delightful prairie. In autumn, when I get sick, I take the book with me to bed in order to gallop my fevers away.

My encounters with books are all clandestine. No one finds out about the tears I shed over David Copperfield or my adventures with Tom Sawyer. In my readings worlds that only I know of are born and die.

When we move downtown, I once more seek refuge in the beckoning whispers of books. I don't like the city.

"Why an apartment?" I plaintively ask anyone who will listen. Corrientes Street bewilders me, makes me cranky, pushes me deeper into my magic cave, the library. There I can create my own space, with my chosen companions: *The Three Musketeers, Martín Fierro, Little Women*. My friends are the letters, upper- and lowercase, at play under the dim light of the reading lamp.

I'm an adolescent eager to learn. Books jump out at me before I choose them. I devour knowledge, take notes, underline paragraphs, read and reread, striving to build a conceptual universe that proves too vast for me. I want to swallow everything whole, without taking time to digest any of it.

Now I'm a college student with a quirk: the desire to read precisely those books that our professors do not recommend. I remember some phrases, certain ideas maybe. The rest is forgotten. Only the books remain. Infinite worlds hidden within infinite signs. One day I don't find what I want, so I decide to write it myself. Since then I've played hide-and-seek among my paragraphs, collecting thoughts, images, moths.

Moths are drawn to the light that kills them. But there are so many that one does not notice—there's always another one, and another, and still one more fluttering around the light bulb. They don't give up.

K-48

I give up. I must surrender, give up my name as if it were a weapon.

"You are K-48. If you forget this, you can forget about ever getting out of here." K-48: first and last name. The code of confinement must be memorized.

You had to memorize the number of the lock for the chain around your ankles, removed only for torture sessions and for bathing. Prisoners without blindfolds were also shackled: that's what marked you as an inmate. Just like in the movies, right? To think that they could shackle you and make you walk around with a ball and chain. The locks that came on and off were not the only ones. The guards were also called locks. There was a lock on your cell door, a lock on your ankles, and another one outside to guard you. And you were called out by your lock number. I'm never going to forget that.

I'm damned if I forget and damned if I don't. Either way, it's all over for me. No more outdoors, no more friends, no more newspapers, no kisses nor moons nor trains. No more.

Lakes, conifer forests, a volcano, all race across the window of the train. Futalaufquen, Huechulaufquen, Lanin. Honeyed words, hot milk and coffee aboard the train that snakes its way south, chocolate at the hostel where high-school campers roll out their sleeping bags. Delicious warm drinks on a cold night in San Martín de los Andes, the toasty refuge teeming with song, mischief, and the anticipation of looking out the window come morning.

I'm awakened by brilliant sunshine, way too bright for my pupils, now used to the smoggy haze. The colors make me dizzy; the glare from the snow on the mountains proves much too strong. The intensity of the light beckons to me, and I set out on a walk. I'm a passenger on a crystal train whose final destination is an oasis, an enormous looking glass pierced by mountains reaching to the center of the earth. There's no one else. I'm all alone before this startling vision of paradise. I run to the lake and look at myself in the mirror. The inverted peaks shatter into myriad fragments the moment the water caresses my lips. I fix on each detail—the smooth edges of the pebbles, the dew, the swaying of a raft by the dock. I sink into a pristine peace that envelops me with earthly arms. I hold the lake in my hands and am suspended in a timeless universe. Boundless. Right then I seal a pact with Nora-to-Come: to remember. I store away these images in the pocket of my memory so I can reach for them whenever necessary. Today I project them onto my closed eyelids to snuggle against the cold.

It is cold

It is cold. Very cold. Cold seeps out from the walls, creeps around the springs of the cot, climbs across the mattress, meanders up my back, and lodges in my neck. It plays along my spine one vertebra at a time, over and back, up and down, down and up, relentlessly. Lethal, grim cold. A pale shaft of light penetrates an invisible crack and cuts the air like a stab. It probes my skin, covered in slime. I want to touch it, but I don't know how. My hands reach for it but collapse lifelessly at my sides. I want to look at it. I lift my head, but it falls down limp. I want to escape this web of wounds and bruises. My shackled feet no longer struggle. Pain moans through my body, repeating obsessively, "You're in a hellhole, disappeared, dis-ap-pear-ed ap-dis-pear-ed." I cover my ears. I curl up and try to sleep, to forget that I am this throbbing, inert thing. I must memorize the code number K-48, K-forty-eight, K-forty plus eight . . .

49, 50, 51

Forty-nine, fifty, fifty-one bars on the enclosure that separates me from the world. I'm confined to a suburb of bandages and antibiotics, the sick face of life: the hospital. Santa Rosa, province of La Pampa, a summer camp instructorship.

Violent storms in January don't make any sense. Rain batters the resigned courtyard tiles, which endure the erosion caused by the drops. Tiles cracked by the merciless November and December sun, punished by the brutal changes in the weather. Our days are spent in the shade of our plans: outdoor activities for whenever it stops raining.

There's only one bar in the area, which boasts a strobe light above the dance floor. Colored rays open infinite fans that burst against dancing shapes. That's why it takes a while to realize that the owner plays, or has, only one record. Night after night, hour after hour, the same syrupy baritone voice, strident at times:

It's better to laugh than to cry / that's how life passes by . . .

Heeding the song's advice, we go out for a drink after dinner. We walk down lanes, deserted monotonous streets lost in the memory of the Viceroyalty, which lead back to our austere bunks in the cavernous old mansion where we're staying. Today it's been raining nonstop since dawn. There's only the murmur of endless drizzle on paving stones, on rooftops. Suddenly the sky lashes out in a rage, slicing time in half. Intermittent claps of thunder roar around us, setting the stage for a cosmic epileptic seizure. A decisive lightning bolt rips open the clouds, unleashing a torrent of water. Airborne curtains, misty veils propelled by gusts, shake the trees out of their stupor.

At the despotic hour of survival my companions crouch for protection under the colonial arcade. I'm incapable of following them. An ancient fatigue pins me to the center of the town square. I lean against columns of water for support. Transparent hands grab me from behind while many others climb up my chest. I become liquid, I don't even breathe.

The medication brings me back to a room that's not the staff dormitory. High, oak-framed windows, monastic-style metal headboards. A nurse approaches to explain the details: rushed to the hospital with pneumonia. I pass the time counting the iron railings that separate me from the world.

It's the day of the Last Judgment. My heart's on a scale in front of the pulpit. The judges are weighing it to assess my conduct on Earth.

"It's very heavy, as if made of lead," they observe, "or simply hardened by many blows." Having successfully reached the required level of maturity, I can now enter the World of Ideas.

"I don't want another world. I want my own! I want a light heart! Please let me go back down to Earth with the others!"

They continue calculating the weight of my ventricles. They're about to return their verdict when I jump the fence and flee at full speed through the streets of Buenos Aires: Santa Rosa, El Tigre, La Boca. Underground labyrinths, nerve-wracking detours clutching at my neck. A fixed stare pursues me. It's the nurse, the fat man with the flabby belly, a surgeon. Metal claws reach for me, tear at my back, close around my throat. I can't cry out. They're pressing on my chest, I cannot breathe. My mouth feels parched, but I hold out until thirst and panic wake me. I ask for water.

Prisoners ask for water, cigarettes, toilets, help. Patience. There's a schedule for everything. Even the cell door has a rhythm of its own. It opens three times a day, once to go to the bathroom and twice to allow for the passage of this concoction they call soup. I set the plate on the cot and try to get some liquid into myself. It's scalding. I blow on each spoonful. "One, two, three, let's see this baby eat her soup. Is she finicky? Baby doesn't want to eat." I do want to, but they remove it. It's time to take it away. More than nourishment, soup is a timepiece for me. It marks my nights and my dawns until I lose track and dwell in unrelieved twilight, in a calendar of my own making with mixed-up pages like infinite eyes.

Death is all eyes

"A woman without hands, without feet, without a head. Death is all eyes," my grandmother used to say. "If she comes ahead of her time, she leaves us a pair of eyes and scurries away before we can catch a glimpse of her. Don't be afraid! Those eyes can see wonders you never imagined. When she comes at the precise moment, though, not a minute before or after, you must follow in silence." Year after year I ask the Three Wise Men to bring me a pair of exotic eyes, but they ignore my request.

"Those are not things for the Three Wise Men to bring. Be patient, you'll get them sometime."

One day I wake up excited: "They're black, Grandma, and so big that they take up my whole head! I can see a thousand things at once!"

With my make-believe eyes I devote myself to exploring people's hidden faces. Beginning with the women I know, I build a house of cards: my ideal woman. For starters, no more housewives like my mother. Forget about bringing up kids, doing the laundry, and feeling like a floor rag. I keep her good-night kiss and her legendary sixth sense.

I discard Grandma's "shoulda done," with which she measures what one did against what one ought to have done. I keep her adventuresome spirit and her branching stories.

My friends' flirtatious ways do not persuade me. I cross them off and emphasize their laughter.

Boring teachers are out. On my list there's only passion for knowledge, and for joy.

With great effort I manage to expel TV personalities.

Fictional heroines stay, with all their virtues minus their hunger for power and wealth.

I attempt to prop up my life with the pillars of this castle of lies, but I bump into my weaknesses, omitted from the list. Full of self-loathing, I scrap it and feel flush with relief. Certain myths no longer weigh me down.

The shackled feet no longer weigh you down; your mind is busy with other urgent matters. Your tangible limits: the walls, the darkness, the cold, the hunger, the pain. More abstract: the moratorium on your life. Most urgent: how to endure what is to follow. Most immediate: the struggle. Most practical: exercise if it gets cold and breathe deeply if you're still here. I take a deep breath: I am still here.

In that place you weren't allowed to speak, you weren't allowed to look around, you weren't allowed to move. The cells had a peephole on the outside. They would approach unexpectedly and look in, and if they found you—even in the darkness—with your blindfold off, or walking about, or exercising, or giving the least sign of being human and showing any hint of resistance, the punishment was swift.

The cell door can burst open at any time:

"Put your blindfold back on, bitch! You're gonna pay for this!"

I pay for wanting to look, I pay for talking, I pay for not wanting to talk. The guards collect for everything and keep the change.

It was Them

It's common in an emergency room for the door to be pushed open and for people to just rush in bringing in a casualty. They yell, "Clear the way!" or "He's bleeding!" and the tension mounts. The stretcher bumps into things; more people barge in, tripping over each other. The noise and commotion create a hectic environment. But these guys never came in pairs; they came in groups of thirty or more, carrying rifles, machine guns, pistols. And they didn't respect the normal procedures for checking in. They'd plunk the person down on the stretcher, let's just say rather carelessly. It was nothing like a father or son or brother bringing in a relative and trying to settle him or her down so that a leg was not hanging out or so the head would be comfortable. They'd fling them in like sacks of potatoes, blood dripping all over. We could tell who they were from the orders that they shouted, from the things they said, from the car radios squawking outside, from the walkie-talkies in their hands, from the instructions and the explanations they gave. "These people were hurt in a confrontation," they'd say, and they'd stay. And no one dared tell them to get out. At most they'd be asked to move aside: "Yes, yes," but they stayed there, right by the wounded. Gradually things would quiet down, a few would walk out and others come back in, a nurse might venture a "Please get that out of my way," to be rid of a machine gun or a rifle lying about. A kind of familiarity seemed to develop after they'd been there a while, hanging around just like at home, and then someone would blurt out, "Listen, man, just step aside, would you? We need some room here!" And we all would slowly regain our composure—the prisoner would be undressed, covered with a sheet, given IVs, blood would be ordered, blood would arrive. "This one needs to be X-rayed, that one goes to surgery," and they'd send someone along with a machine gun to the X-ray lab or the operating room.

The thing is that the emergency room had never been under police jurisdiction, and yet it was clear that the people giving the orders and preventing a clinical history from being drawn up were those bringing in the casualties. If one of us, pretending not to be aware of what was happening, approached and said, "Let's have your name," one of them would intervene immediately: "No, no, get away, no notes!" No one asked why, or who you were. It was understood. It was Them.

SCIFO MÓDICA'S anonymity lasted until last May. On the fifteenth of that month the Federal Police inaugurated a Center for the Care of Victims of Sexual Violence, a branch of the Center for the Orientation of Victims, chaired by Scifo Módica. His picture was published in the newspapers, and his face was familiar to some disappeared ex-prisoners. It was "Scorpion," from the Athletic Club.—*Página 12*, 16 July 1996

The electric prod opens gashes, which the guards close with utmost care so that they can be opened again.

They opened the door of our crafts workshop, where we kept our tools—polishers, different instruments, among them a dentist's drill used for burnishing rings. "Mmmm, what a terrific prod!" I heard them say.

Thanks to the prod, I end up in the infirmary.

THERE WAS MEDICAL CARE, but it was only for people close to death from excessive torture, for those whom they wanted to keep on torturing. They were taken to the infirmary, treated, given IVs, and then returned to the torture chamber. One of the prisoners was in charge of the infirmary.—CONADEP

The prisoner or the nurse or the doctor in charge is approaching. I can tell by the booming echo of his footsteps. The room must be large and right by a street, judging by the roar of cars. A splash of light penetrates my closed eyelids, while an unhurried voice accompanies the cotton digging around my wounds. A soothing, serene voice that could belong to any nurse in any provincial hospital. I answer without being asked: "I don't know anything, I'm not involved, I don't know."

I know nothing

What do I know? I only know that I know nothing. I'm a figment of the imagination, an abstraction. I read no newspapers, find TV disgusting. I read novels and listen to the Beatles. I must really like them, since I don't understand a word they say. But it's not necessary to read the papers to get a feel for reality: the swing set where I played as a child faced a barrio where tin roofs form a collage among eucalyptus trees and garbage. At sixteen I'm a teacher and must teach barefoot kids to say "shoe." We have well-educated beggars here; they know their English.

"I'm a teacher," I told the milico.
"Yeah, sure, raising people's consciousness," he cut in.
"Don't be ridiculous," I shot back. "Can't you see that this is a kindergarten?"

In Argentina one has to be really dumb to look and not see. It takes little effort to come face to face with the upside-down world. At seventeen I start college. Since I'm a good listener and have a schizophrenic aunt, I major in psychology: the so-called Red Forum, the haven of infiltrators, the core of foreign ideologies.

WE'RE NOT FACING an adversary that fights to defend a flag, or a nation, or to protect its borders. Our enemy is nothing like that. It's simply an army of ideologues whose headquarters can be anywhere in Europe, America, or Asia.—General Acdel Vilas

During the day students act like students: they go up and down halls, attend classes, answer questions, take notes, go to the library. Professors act like professors: they arrive late, forget their notes, improvise, ask questions, give tests. Only the whispers that can be heard backstage—petitions, denunciations, accusations, admonitions, exhortations—give the lie to this routine. But what is whispered by night refutes what goes on during the day: assemblies are organized, demands formulated, support sought, votes solicited, resolutions passed.

The curtain falls in mid-act. The whispers have bodies; the bodies scream and scramble to escape; they jump out of windows, climb over rooftops. Some disappear down alleyways that lead to subways, taxis, or buses; others escape in pairs and plunge into hotel rooms rented by the hour; a few sit in cafés, all the better to watch the performance.

Blue uniforms control the doors of the building. A police van is parked right in front. Massive motorcycles, connected by radio to an invisible but powerful headquarters, ride rings around it. At the signal the uniforms spew tear gas. The students respond by setting fire to desks and blackboards. The rear doors of the van open up and devour those who are flushed out, expelled by the gas. Other bodies flee through the smoke toward safety.

When the blue uniforms and the vans show up during the first act, though, the scene takes place outdoors. Thousands of unpaid extras march down the street, waving homemade signs. The columns of paid extras march toward them with better costumes and props: they wear uniforms and carry weapons.

Carrying their regulation weapons, uniformed forces come to our factory to demand a thousand fireproof bricks, the most expensive kind. I tell them that I'm not authorized to give things away, that I've got to check. The leader of the operation gets furious: "That's no way to help your country," he says and storms out. On the following Monday he returns, and I tell him that we're going to give them tiles instead of bricks. The guy insists that they want something else, that this is not alms, or a gift, or even a donation, but a contribution to the nation. He goes ahead and takes the three hundred tiles anyway, and as he leaves, he stares at a Mafalda cartoon poster that reads, "There is no way for someone

to amass a fortune without first grinding others into flour." Two
days later my brother and I are kidnapped for, according to them,
loading the truck with . . . rifles!

The arms, rifles; the teeth, bullets; the eyes, targets. That's
what we thought, but they're more sinister still: regular guys,
wearing suits and ties. Just like any office worker, bank employee, or teacher. People like us, except that their work consists
of asking questions and softening up the prisoner with scientifi-
cally devised methods. That is, unless they're in a hurry.

YOU WANNA KNOW how we went about interrogating a prisoner. A lot depended on how rushed we were, on the time of
day. For example, if it was about two in the afternoon, we would
have to work fast . . . because there might be a meeting in an
hour and a half, and in order not to miss it, the interrogation
would be sped up by using torture or electric shocks.—Julián
the Turk, *Página 12*, 2 May 1995

IF ANYWHERE IN THE WORLD well-paid, full-time positions to
carry out torture were advertised, how many applications
would they receive?—Jacobo Timerman

How a history professor speaks with a lady:
"Señora, I assure you this kind of work has its drawbacks. You
can't imagine how hard it was for me when my very best student
confessed his sympathy for socialism. I was his history professor,
but still my first obligation was to the Army. And so I had to inform them, as is expected of us. They took him away; it was a real
pity. Doing the right thing isn't always easy."
    The lady turns her back on him while fixing some coffee.
They've been at her house for hours and need a break. She's in a
somewhat awkward position, not only because the kitchen is
narrow but also because a longhaired youth follows her from the
cupboard to the table, keeping the muzzle of his pistol pressed

against the nape of her neck. Occasionally he brushes against her arm or her buttocks, and she turns to ice. He follows her around, his hand steady, unfalteringly macho. The professor takes off his leather jacket and gets comfortable while the boys finish turning over and cutting open a few easy chairs just in case there are any documents hidden in them. No luck, it's just filling, and the cheap kind to boot.

"Coffee's ready. Come and have some. You fellows must be tired."

The lady strains to be agreeable so that they won't get cranky and slash up what's left of her furnishings. The professor takes a few sips of coffee and orders a blond thug to go raid the house that the lady has so kindly mentioned. Meanwhile the lady knits, trying to stay calm. She has swallowed so much saliva, there are so many bitter words floating in that whitish liquid that burns holes in her trachea and in her stomach, that her bladder is now ablaze and she urgently needs to pee. She's overcome by the intensity of this need, even if it means doing it right in the middle of the living room.

"Please excuse me, I've got to use the bathroom."

The professor signals subtly with his index finger, setting in motion a short but hefty character, who puts his coffee down on the white china plate, takes the machine gun from the corner, and strides determinedly after the shadow etched against the wall. She and her shadow go through the door, with the armed midget following right behind. She is not sure that she can do it in front of this warlike statue, with a gun aimed at her temple. What would it be like to die in a "shoot-out," to have your brains blown out while peeing, and to show up like that on the front page of the newspaper? Of course, in this country of ours such an episode would never make the news. What's it like, then, to pee in front of a soldier primed for action?

A warm and liberating river flows between her legs, and she no longer knows, or cares, if the warrior is aiming at her, or if the musical tinkle will arouse his instincts, or if he'll let go of the trigger to grab hold of his penis in the heat of battle. She's no longer there with him, she's alone with her body in a corner of her house, with her waterfall of words, which will be flushed down labyrinths of pipes and start on their journey south, moving unimpeded under barrios, under streets, toward the river, and from there spreading to every shore.

Another script

Backstage, another script is rehearsed every day, around the clock. There are muffled cries, slamming doors; sometimes nothing's heard at all. What's going on?

You have to guess, pick up subtle signs, keep very quiet or you won't hear a thing. It's experimental theater. I miss rehearsals, and they get annoyed: this comrade doesn't want to commit, she's trapped in her middle-class limitations and doesn't strive to get beyond them.

I don't want a leading role; even bit parts seem much too demanding. I'm always improvising, can't seem to memorize the script, but they insist on casting me, on seducing me with promises of revolution. I believe in utopias too, but not in giving up my life as a way of life. Perhaps the suburbs of heroism are not my favorite neighborhoods, or I'm suffering from premature old age. I keep a certain distance that prevents me from joining the chorus of protests, reading pamphlets sprinkled with calls to arms, and betting with certainty on the creation of a better world. I bet nonetheless, eager for victory though unconvinced of it. It's impossible to be young in 1977 and not bet on the creation of the New Man, on change.

Change your first name, change your last name, change every-
thing, a friend told me when we met after things had changed. And
I changed, just like the song that says everything changes.

Everything changed when we heard that shot, as crystal-clear
as the second that precedes death. It was evening, and during the
rally in the streets of barrio Once, we had unwittingly gotten too
close to a police station. When we realized they had fired on us,
we ran. I went down Viamonte toward Pueyrredón Street. It happened there, slicing the night in two. Clear as a premonition. I
felt it as one feels horror the first time. He was buried the following day. Emilio Jáuregui—a name, a shot, an undying profile into
which I peered apprehensively, afraid of finding out too much. I
was afraid. My friends were too, but they tamed their fear. Some
got weapons. It was absurd to face weapons without weapons,
but I was incapable of carrying death in my hand. Even if they de-
served it.

I take several years plotting my escape. Too many. Before the
last curtain call I am to tiptoe off the stage into a waiting taxi for
the final exit, the airport. No one will notice. I'm not important
enough. I was wrong: someone noticed.

They call the shots

They notice and keep track, come and go as they please, because
they call the shots. Circa 1976: upright citizens, their voices spent
begging for help, bang on doors of military barracks. Bankers,
entrepreneurs, doctors, certain students, a few housewives, a lot
of bureaucrats, all fed up with the fact that in this country the
rules of the game are not being followed. Let's have the military
keep us on a short leash for a while. It's been done before, and it
wasn't so bad. Let them wipe out the enemies, deal with their
tantrums with a firm hand. The Army will take power on behalf
of the people in order to finish off the subversives.

Operation Independence, the model for what was to come, was launched on the night of 9 February 1975 in the province of Tucumán. Its stated purpose was to "neutralize and/or annihilate subversive elements," but they ended up massacring left and right even before the military coup. We were out as usual, oblivious to everything, nonchalantly having a drink at a sidewalk café. Army trucks started rolling in, and between sips of whiskey we observed, "Take a look at what's coming our way." My friend's brother was in hiding, I had already been in jail, and still we were totally blind to what was brewing. He was taken soon after. We never fathomed what was happening. For instance, in 1974 we used to work through the night at the People's Newspaper. *We'd hear bombs go off, but our main concern was who'd cover the next story rather than the explosions, which continued until dawn. We just didn't have a clue. I don't think anyone did. "This is going to turn into a bloodbath," a policeman had said to my father, but we simply couldn't conceive of it. When you're surrounded by terror you just don't realize it: you go to bed with terror, you live with terror; it somehow gets incorporated into your routine. And when it's over, you look back and wonder, how could we have endured this, how could we bear to get a call in the morning and be told, "You know what? One of your friends was taken away last night," and say, "Shit, that's awful," and just hang up the phone?*

Let's talk on the phone and play in the woods while the wolf's not around. *Is the wolf there? / I'm putting on my socks!* And my underwear with the reinforced crotch, to keep my balls in place. All set. They've put on gloves, boots, jackets; they have their regulation manuals, instructions, tanks, weapons. Let's get on with National Reorganization. Let's straighten out the country (a straitjacket?). It's no easy task—dissolve, forbid, burn, rule, clean up. The fun of the game gets compounded.

Step on a crack, break your mother's back.

COMMUNIQUÉ NUMBER 19. 24 MARCH 1976

Citizens are hereby informed that the Military Junta has re-solved that whosoever distributes or in any way propagates information or images from, or attributed to, illegal groups or persons engaged in terrorism or subversive activities of any kind shall be imprisoned indefinitely. Whosoever distributes such information with the purpose of interfering with the activities of the armed forces, the security forces, or the police or in any way tarnishing their image shall be imprisoned for a period of up to ten years.

In order not to interfere with the activities of the armed forces, the police, or other security forces or to tarnish their image, one must speak with propriety and use an ample vocabulary:

Fight the enemy: kill and/or disappear children, youths, adults, or senior citizens. Pregnant women can also be sucked up.

Suck up: kidnap. Hellhole: natural habitat of the kidnapped person.

Kidnapped person: terrorist.

Terrorist: political militant with ideas contrary to those of the military.

Ideas of the military: to safeguard the Nation, the Family, and Property.

Property: universal concept that includes one's own and that belonging to subversives.

Subversives: said of all antisocial and disruptive elements who will be fitted with blindfolds.

Blindfold: handkerchief or rag placed over the eyes of subversives to keep them from seeing their tormentors.

Tormentors: forces specializing in interrogation methods.

Interrogation methods: prod, submersion, grill, etc. The list is too long. In the Republic of Argentina the son of the illustrious writer Leopoldo Lugones invented the electric prod.

Prod: sharp-tipped conduit for electrical current kept in the operating room.

Operating room: space designed for the interrogation of subversives before sending them to the tube.

Tube: cell measuring 8 feet by 5 feet where subversives can rest under the supervision of guards.

Guards: Shark, Viper, Tiger, Blondie, Turk, Belly, Lightbulb, Pacifier, Angel, Colors, Scorpion. Not regular cops but members of Special Task Forces.

Special Task Forces: groups of individuals devoted to the annihilation of the enemy and to the appropriation of the spoils of war.

Spoils of war: all sorts of goods, including real estate, appropriated after every battle by military personnel.

Military personnel: officials belonging to the intelligence services.

Intelligence: word that means obedience.

Due obedience: concept employed in case there is a public trial, in order to pass the responsibility along to one's superior officer.

Superior officer: one who has nothing to confess, to add, or to regret.

"I HAVE NOTHING TO REGRET," declares General Lambruschini.

"God has already forgiven me," declares General Agosti.

"Twenty-nine persons, supposedly disappeared, are included in the lists of survivors of the recent earthquake in Mexico," says the defense lawyer for General Viola.

"Marxist agitators are running scared," declares General Viola.

"I have nothing to add," declares General Anaya.—*La Nación*, October 1985

Now it's my turn to take the stand in a more civilized way: sitting in front of a typewriter that can either record my words or copy a cooking recipe. Same difference. A truly official deposition, so official that I must sign it blindly at the bottom of the page. I scribble something to signify approval of this bureaucratic farce. They're so efficient: Everything is neatly filed. They take note of those who enter and exit, their distinguishing physical traits, their histories, contacts, ideas. Of course, at times a gust of wind throws their papers into disarray, the facts get mixed up, things get messy.

What a mess! No one seems to have ordered my transfer. Some women from the provincial penitentiary call the Federal Police, who assure them that they have not ordered my transfer. Next they call the state police, who assure them that they also have not ordered my transfer. Then they call the intelligence services: no way have they ordered my transfer. They finally call a regiment in Formosa, who assures them that in fact the military has ordered my transfer and that I should remain confined right there. It must have been about three in the afternoon, but I was exhausted. They shoved me into a cell that was no bigger than 8 feet by 4 feet, and I must have fallen asleep. When I came to, my water had broken and I started yelling for help. One of the guards came in, and I told her that I wanted to be taken to a maternity ward because my water had broken. It was obvious that I was telling the truth because my clothes were soaked.

I bid farewell to my clothes as if they were old friends—corduroy slacks and a printed blouse. I'm given some others that reek of jail, of dampness. Shirt, pants, clothes belonging to one of the departed. Confiscated garments, they call them.

It's not only that my clothes are soaked but that I'm about to give birth. Still the midwife says no, to which I counter yes, I've already had a daughter and I know when I'm about to give birth. I

warn her that I'm Rh-negative and tell her about the shot to neu-
tralize it. She makes a note of it but does nothing. She goes out to
feed her ducks. At about eight that night, when I realize that I'm
fully dilated, I scream even louder. It's a liberating scream that
breaks with all those inhibitions imposed by this culture on
women. My guard has the nurse called. She shuffles down the hall
the moment I start pushing. She orders me to walk to the delivery
room. I tell her I can't, that the baby is coming fast, but she insists
she is not going to help me have the baby here. So I get up, with my
legs spread wide, my hand on my son's head, which is coming
right out, and like that I make my way down corridors I've forgot-
ten to the delivery room. There she has me lie down on a bed and
starts to take some blood samples. I beg her to hurry and repeat
that the baby is coming fast. Finally, she reacts and helps him out.
My son is born with the cord wrapped twice around his neck, with-
out a cry or even a whimper.

Without a cry or even a whimper, I hand my contact lenses
over to the guards. It makes no difference since it's forbidden to
take off the blindfold even while sleeping. A blindness infused
with screams—from boys, from women, from men. Disjointed
echoes that hover in the void. Madness.

To each her own

For me, madness has a name. It's Berta. She has blue eyes in
which I love to get lost and hands that spin to the tune of *tick,*
tock, goes the clock / to each her own measure / and if we don't,
and if we don't / we must forfeit a treasure.

We always played forfeits with my aunt. We had to move our
hands, wave our arms like shoemakers, like washerwomen, as if
we were ironing to lyrics that nailed, washed, and ironed at a
dizzying tempo. Whoever mixed up the trades had to forfeit a
treasure. You could always settle your debt by doing three somer-
saults, or jumping like a frog. But it was different for Berta. Her

punishment was the madhouse, for inventing rules that grown-ups did not understand. Now your hands do not move to the tune of our music; they're barely up to waving from the window that frames thirty years of captivity, thirty years between that softly padded lap that used to cradle me and this tired and lonely lap, thirty years between your black chignon and your white one, between the bedroom window through which you used to jump out into the open and the window of the hospital room.

They labeled as crazy your habit of taking trains all the way to the end of the line, heading south in any open freight car to look at the pampas, that golden sea dotted with cows and farm gates. Those rides took you to out-of-the-way towns, where your family eventually caught up with you, aided by clues that you left along the way.

One day we are invited to celebrate your engagement: your boyfriend is coming from Montevideo. Intrigued, we gather around a table laden with canapés and tea sandwiches, eagerly anticipating his arrival. Hours pass, and the guest of honor doesn't show. The others begin to get impatient, to concoct explanations. Teodora goes up to you and asks if you have any idea what might have happened.

"You know perfectly well what happened," you shoot back irately, and you send everyone home.

The following week, eager to make amends, you invite Teodora to dinner. After all, it's not worth fighting over a man. You serve minestrone soup followed by a main course of steak and salad. For dessert, ice cream sprinkled with ground-up glass. Since then your home has been the psychiatric hospital, a cubical universe of wall, wall, wall, ceiling, floor, and window.

Berta is allowed visitors once a week. Her brothers come once a month, for two hours. They bring her hand-me-down clothes, cookies, occasionally a magazine. Since they never accept her invitation to tea, they never discover that she eats and drinks everything out of the same dented tin cup, that she stirs her *mate cocido* with the same spoon that she eats with, because she has only one. She's used to it; she asks for nothing.

Ask for nothing

We asked our families to bring us things in jail, but it wasn't easy. Sometimes visits took place in a room with a glass partition, or with steel bars. Other times we had to kneel on church pews set across from each other in a huge room. Even though we had to shout to be heard, we took advantage of the opportunity to ask for things.

No one asks the guard for anything, not even when the doors to the cells are open. I just hope he'll go away. His steps are heard down the corridor, firm and determined, on their way to deal with some other prisoner's dirt. The doors are left open, as if it were possible to air out the stench of urine and dampness that permeates everything. I want to pull my blindfold down, but even this simple gesture fills me with dread.

I was filled with dread every time a guard's footsteps echoed in the corridor. Everyone was afraid to be taken back for more torture. Ironically, sometimes you wanted to go out just to stretch your legs or use the bathroom, but at the same time you didn't, because that simple act exposed you to the glances of your captors and to anything and everything that popped into their minds. You wavered between these two options.

The mind gradually shrinks, and your world becomes limited to when they open the door, when they close it, what you eat today, what you'll eat tomorrow, when you're punished, and when you're not. Those were the things that most mattered to me. When your life gets so small, you forget where you are, who you are. You're grateful for any friendly gesture, for a plate of decent food; you're happy to be outdoors for a bit. Thinking becomes pointless.

I have all the time in the world to think, but I don't. I lower my blindfold. I make out a face to go with that pair of legs. I pull on the corners of my eyes, fingers to the aid of my nearsightedness, and recover the focus on the screen: gaunt, red hair, beard.

"Where are we?" I venture with a thread of voice.

"In a hellhole, top security."

"For how long?"

"I've been here six months. All my *compañeros* have been killed."

Footsteps echo. Blindfolds are hastily replaced and our words silenced. In the cells of not being, speaking is strictly forbidden.

Fortunately, screaming is not forbidden because your voice booms loud and clear: "You've reappeared, Norita. You haven't changed at all!" Your words chisel into my surprise. I arrive out of breath, bewildered by the pilgrimage down senseless corridors, always the wrong ones, echoing with requests for food, money, cigarettes.

It's me, Aunt Berta, I'm the one who can feel the sting of your thirty years of mildewed walls reeking of reheated leftovers, of vacant stares from inmates locked up in towers of fear, of nurses trained to inject the prescribed dose of sedatives. Whatever it takes to keep them well within the circle of old slippers, shuffling along the colorless mosaic of madness. Madness is a form of salvation—an escape from logic, an anchor cast somewhere farther back, where normal people never venture. It's a form of barter: turn the knight into a bishop, move across the board diagonally, and keep on going. You decree that the chessboard doesn't exist, that the pawns are for you or against you, that the queen has fled and the king is stalking you. So no one wants to play. You're left all alone, surrounded by disembodied voices, voices that other players cannot hear. And if by chance they did, they would cover their ears and go out to buy locks and bars and electricity and sedatives to control you. Everything must be made to fit within those seductive cushions of rationality.

Eight beds and no closet, no night table, no place to keep whatever it is you have, no room to be who you are. Your world is a prison where polite, smiling guards wear white. Within that setting you give piano recitals and lectures on international politics, trying to get the others unplugged from the TV set.

"Nothing interests them, those dummies. And they don't believe me when I say that I won awards for architectural design. They can't imagine that anyone has horizons beyond their own."

You take my arm and gesticulate while we walk around the forlorn gardens that surround your lucidity. At the end of visiting hours you walk me down to the bus stop.

"Are you allowed to go out?"

"Sure. They know I wouldn't get far. Where would I go? There are some who try to run away and others who jump out the windows. I gave up. In the end they always win."

Father to daughter after a game of chess:
"Dear, you have to learn to lose."
"But, Papa, can't you see that I already know how to lose? What I need to do is learn to win!"—Pablo Conti

They're not going to win. I walk back and forth in the cell, even if it is only two steps long, even if I bump into walls, even if the weight of the shackles on my legs frightens me, even if my whole body hurts, even if they want to enslave my soul.

THE DISCIPLINE was rigorous, and the chains bruised my ankles and kept me from moving more than 10 inches. Our eyes were covered with a blindfold that was like glasses made of cloth, bound tightly over the eyes. . . . We were not allowed to talk or move and were forced to always be sitting or lying down. . . . The guards walked about in sneakers and barged in unexpectedly to see if we were standing up or had taken off the blindfold because even inside the cells our eyes had to remain covered.—CONADEP

They took me to a cell known as "the tube" because it was so long and narrow. It was barely as wide as a door, and it had two benches, one with a foam-rubber mattress. Above the metal door there was a small opening onto a long corridor. I was taken there and kept in total isolation for a long time.

Perhaps I'll manage to stay sane if I cover myself with the foam-rubber mattress and inhale the cell's dampness to oblivion.

Or it might be better to sing a song. *Letter L, dear friend of mine / sign of luscious liberty / why do you go with others / leaving me behind?*

How do I earn an *L*, that elegant letter worn by the privileged few who make it back up the stairs? Not even with lies. Even if I knew something and told them, they might still finish me off. They're volatile, unpredictable. You can never figure out their reasoning, which is always fixed, never good. Upright reasons, erect, unbending. For better or worse, I was never given the opportunity to confess, not even before the prudish ear of a holy frock. And now there are priests here passing out blessings, but my quarter of an hour is up. I heard one of them walk by. He spoke with the guy in the cell next to mine and repeatedly told him that he'd been guilty of keeping the wrong company but that he could mend his ways.

AFTER THE ABDUCTION [of her husband] Smith's wife . . . had an audience with President Videla to ask his help. "He received me with a rosary in his hand. 'I've just finished my prayers,' he told me. Later he said my husband's disappearance might have been a 'self-kidnapping,' or that maybe he was held outside the country, although he admitted the possibility it might have been the work of parapolice or paramilitary forces. 'The thing is, your husband is too involved in the union.'"—Andersen, *Dossier Secreto*

I was in the teacher's union when I was kidnapped. The first thing they asked me was who my spiritual guide was, my confessor. I told them I had no spiritual guide, that whenever I wanted to confess I went to the first priest I found in church. What I never told them was that, thank God, I'm a confirmed atheist and that I went to church only to talk liberation theology with young priests. They made me feel right at home.

"GET OUT of here, this is my home," Father Mai blurted out.

"We thought this was the house of God," cut in Hebe de Bonafini, flanked by thirteen other Mothers of the Plaza de Mayo.

"You trouble-makers . . . let me speak," he barked back as a group of about twenty policemen entered the cathedral (and the ambulances got ready to take the women away for disorderly conduct).

"Why didn't you speak out when they took away 30,000 *desaparecidos?*"—*Página 12*, 9 July 1996

The disappeared are forbidden to speak. One calls out to the guard: he wants to be taken to the bathroom. It's not allowed outside of scheduled hours. He has to soil himself and will be beaten for it, and he will continue to soil himself until he's been beaten to a pulp. I'm beginning to understand. The first person singular is not conjugated here. What's the use, if they're going to kill us all.

"Are they going to kill us?"

"If you get transferred, they kill you; if you spend a night on the main floor, they let you go," my neighbor whispers.

T/L. Our destiny hangs on two letters.

The letter **T** *was stamped on the records of Graciela and Gerardo sometime after November '77. Occasionally they would also* *add a cross . . . I saw it when I worked in the office filing papers. They had originally removed my blindfold so I could fix stolen electrical appliances. That's why they didn't "off" me, because they could continue to use me. I was free skilled labor.*

They are the keepers of the keys to the alphabet and to the cemetery gate. As if that weren't enough, they know the date of our end.

I can see, I can see

Today is 17 December, my birthday. Too bad that I have to spend it sick in bed with a sore throat. To top it off, my party was canceled. I bet they'll postpone it till January and then simply lump it together with Gerardo's. A two-tier cake with many more candles, with more icing on his side. Luckily, my aunt gave me a doll. She's black, with big bulging eyes, and she's older than I am.

I can see, I can see / What can you see? Something / Something what? Something marvelous / What color? / Green!

I guessed right. They're taking me out. My fever is down. I ask Mama to let me wear my Sunday shoes and my yellow dress, which looks so good against the greens in the plaza. We drive over there: the doll, Mama, Papa, and I. We park in front of a gray building. No grass, no flowers, no swings, no slides in sight.

"What are we doing here?"

"We're just going to visit for a little while."

Two firm hands push me toward the main entrance. I don't want to go in, but we're already inside. Mama's knocking on the door.

A fan of white smocks opens before my eyes like a peacock's tail. No one goes with me. The doll too stays behind. The smocks have hands. They trap me in a net of white sheets. They tie me to an enormous chair that leans back, leaving me with my head down and my legs up in the air. I scream, but they do not stop.

They're not listening. I can't move or close my mouth. A harsh light bears down on my face. A machine larger than all their hands is coming toward me. It presses down on my tongue and moves around my throat. I'm going to throw up. They release me so that I can spit blood out into the sink. I spit out my birthday.

I fight back with the only weapon I have: silence. My parents try to buy my forgiveness with an ice-cream cone. They defend themselves with excuses that make them sound like worn-out battle horses: "We just did what the doctor told us. We didn't know what they were going to do to you." All those bitter-tasting syllables dig into me and turn into stones in my stomach. I don't know what to do with my resentment, now a nasty knot in my throat. Little by little it loosens up, and I start speaking to them. But never about what happened. I'm left with a scarred soul, an invisible mark that will grow with the years and become a scab. Having thus learned my lesson, I'm prepared to educate scores of new generations eager to obey the commands of adults.

"Attennn-tion! J 08 and 09! One, two, aaaand threeee!"

I don't know what this is all about. Since my cell door is open, I huddle by its frame. A viper snakes its metallic body down the corridor in front of me, but I'm not ordered to react. I'm frozen at attention, with all my neurons on alert.

You had to be on alert when they said "from cell such and such to cell thus and thus," or according to our letters and numbers. You had to file out and join the train.

The two-legged train goes by, leaving no audible traces, and I'm left alone, terrified, in my useless military stance, on the verge of splintering into a multitude of fears.

It was terrifying when they put animals in my cell. It was an isolation cell where they kept me awake. Whenever I fell asleep, they'd throw water on me and then send in dogs. Those bastards even had a ferret, a really nasty little beast. It's similar to the weasel, which feeds on rats and other small rodents, but when it gets hungry, it will attack humans in places like the earlobe or the nose. That ferret really messed up my nose, nibbling on it whenever I dozed off. The guards had it in there for the sheer fun of it. They cracked up laughing during these episodes. That was the scariest part of all.

Infinite fears are born and die day after day, on any street of any neighborhood, at the university, even in one's own home. Rolled-up fears, sticky fears, dull or voluptuous fears, succulent ones in all brands and flavors.

We could only concentrate on ourselves by blocking out our fears, by blocking out the color or the smell of the risk of falling into their hands. The typical student went to the university, that fabled island of democracy, carrying a notebook full of addresses that he or she was supposed to swallow in the bathroom in case of danger. Students had to pass the main door, monitored by intruders in blue; go into the classrooms under the surveillance of intruders in civilian clothes; participate in assemblies controlled by intruders of both kinds. And then return home, and avoid being followed by the usual intruders.

There we were, for better or worse, getting our tactics and strategies all jumbled up at times, pegging them right on occasion, always on the verge of revolution. A few carried weapons, not so much in order to attack the cops as to defend themselves from militants of different stripes during the heated student elections. That was before the coup, when Isabelita Perón sent troops into the university and the dean had to go underground. Can you imagine the dean of a university living underground? In the end he had to seek asylum in the Mexican Embassy. We used to consume megadoses of magical realism. But some paid a high price. After assemblies the cops would stand at the door, and we had to parade out in single file. They just pointed their fingers: this one out, that one in, and many of the kids who'd spoken out went straight from there into state custody, caught like flies, sucked up as if through the hose of a vacuum cleaner. They kept many until '86 or '87, well after the dictatorship had ended.

I remember one instance in particular: A group of students went to the dean's office to demand that the police be removed from campus. Only two were allowed in. I volunteered and dragged along a friend, who had little option but to follow. As soon as the door closed behind us the others were ushered out. Instead of the dean we found his office crawling with cops. It's like with mosquitoes—you never know where they come from, but it's clear what they're after. I had a somewhat reassuring thought: if they tried to take me away, there'd be witnesses all along the hall, down the stairs, and across the main lobby. I still thought they used the front door! We were rushed down a spiral staircase and straight into a police van.

From hole to hole

WE WERE TAKEN to the bathroom three times a day. The bathrooms were about 100 feet from the cell block. We marched in single file, in groups of ten, holding on to one another's shoulders. Most of the time we couldn't take care of our needs because as soon as we arrived, they'd give the order to return to the cell block, or they'd beat us, or they'd allow just two or three minutes for all of us to use the bathroom. They also gave us water there, but usually no time to drink it.—CONADEP

"From the cell to the bathroom we choo-choo train along," a silky voice tells me, the first woman to speak to me here. A prisoner turned guard? A real guard?

"Whenever you hear them call out 'Number One!' it means you must turn; when they say 'Two!' put your hands on the shoulders of the person ahead of you; on 'Three!' march. C'mon, hurry. Don't let them notice you're falling behind." I follow.

"We're here. Now squat."

They give the order to begin the countdown. I fall in line: about face, three, two, one. This isn't any cute little choo-choo train; it's more like a slimy, reeking centipede. Forty pairs of legs shuffling along from hole to hole.

THERE WAS a disguised entrance to the basement, which had no ventilation or daylight. The temperature was between 104 and 113°F in summer and very cold in winter. It was very damp; the walls and floor were constantly dripping water. . . . Kitchen, washroom, and showers, these with an opening in the wall through which the guards would check out the women's asses.—*Nunca Más*

We strip and run to the showers still wearing our chains, pushing, stomping, kicking. It's usually the women who get pawed. The guards rate us as soon as we start to pull down our pants. Quality control is not an arbitrary or individual process; they consult among themselves before passing judgment. The ass of the third one, the legs of this one, the tits of the first one in line—one hundred points. Any other bids? Going once, going twice . . .

"Hey baby, do I have something for you!"

The soap is slippery. Watch out: it mustn't fall outside the imaginary square on the tiles. Look only at your own feet, never lift your eyes; get dressed again, fast; you must not lag behind or slip.

"Watch out, blondie, you're gonna get it!"

Ice-cold lashes on your back. Better enjoy it, this might just be your last time under the water.

MAYBE once a week they took us to the showers . . . makeshift ones at that, just two pipes with holes through which water dripped. We had about a minute, more or less, to wash in groups of eight, get out, dry off. There were between a hundred and a hundred and forty of us, and five or six rags that served as towels for everyone.—CONADEP

Everything's for everyone, even the screams in the night. As a rule, you don't make your way up in life here, only down, sinking lower and lower until there's only night, the infinity of night, the rock bottom of night. A night resonant with moans and footsteps, with impatient knocks on doors that open onto nothingness. The door is flung open but not on schedule. It's not time for the bathroom or for the soup.

I'm appropriately attired, wearing my blindfold. I've learned to obey. They take me. Stand up, walk down the corridor, careful. We climb some steps. Another unexpected movement upwards. To where? Fresh air, like in a patio or courtyard. Like an evening breeze.

"Wait here until you're called."

THE ATHLETIC CLUB: this camp was under the direct orders of the high command of the Federal Police and functioned as the headquarters of their intelligence operations, but it was also used by different task forces, who took their disappeared there.—CONADEP

Could this be an Army barrack? Police Headquarters?

The police changed over time, but you always had to be on guard. Many years ago my old man had a drinking buddy who was an officer. I knew him too, since I'd often tag along to have a ham and cheese sandwich and a soda at the bar. Once I was arrested for passing out pamphlets and ended up at the station. They greeted me with punches and kicks, as usual.

At some point this officer comes in and says, "Stop it, stop it! What's going on here? What happened, kid? What are you doing here?" He even puts his hand on my shoulder. Since I'm bleeding,

*he leads me to a sink with a faucet. "Here, wash up." As I'm wash-
ing I feel a blow, and my face and teeth crash into the faucet. He
has whacked me with every intention of smashing my face.*

*I turn around and stare at him in disbelief. He keeps repeating,
"What are you looking at? What are you looking at me for?"*

A voice warns me: "Look out, the place is crawling with
guards. Behave yourself." The floor sounds different from the
one downstairs; security measures seem more relaxed.

It seems that they won't push us around here; at most we'll
be ignored.

"Yes sir, Lieutenant."

"Come here, Corporal."

"At once, sir."

A military base? Clicking typewriters, a lot of coming and going. And other prisoners: the sporadic shuffling of chains against
the floor is the Morse code of the nameless.

*Before even asking my name they gave me a good beating;
then, around nine in the evening they brought me to an office at
Police Headquarters. I was badly hurt, barefoot, with no belt to
hold up my pants; there was a half-open box of crackers and a
thermos of coffee. In the morning, civilian employees started arriving. They didn't seem to be bothered at all by the spectacle I presented, and they treated me as if I were a flower vase adorning the
corner of an apartment.*

The threshold

A police station? The shackles hurt my ankles, the tiles are ice-
cold. I can't stand still. Perhaps it's the others, or the breeze, or
the sudden expectation of being on the threshold of freedom. I
don't know what it is. Something in the air speaks through me.

"Excuse me, sir. Could I please move around a bit? I'm cold."

A mortal silence cuts the space in half: They're on one side, all of them, stunned. I'm on the other, with my flawless instinct for saying the wrong thing. They're going to get their kicks harassing me. What will they do?

"All right," he decrees flatly.

We used to spend time at a friend's who lived right by a police station. His yard and the Eighth Police Precinct's were back to back. He told me they could hear both music and screams coming from there, that they were torturing people. It was the time of Perón, the fifties. We were vaguely aware that the political police were operating there, behind that gate. Those were Special Forces, which later became part of the Federal Police.

They said I could. I can hardly believe that I'm given permission to do anything, but I stand up and begin to move my numb body. I manage to coordinate my movements despite the shackles. I stand on tiptoe, stretch my arms up toward the ceiling. "Bravooo! Let's see that once more! Look guys, *Swan Lake*! Keep it up!" The voices draw nearer as I continue; steadily, obsessively, I continue. "Now *The Nutcracker*!" I keep up the rhythm, and a one, and a two. "Do *The Tarantella*!" And a three, and a four. "Go for *Blue Danube*!" And I forget about the chorus, and up and down, and over and over, where their sneers cannot touch me, and one and two, I'm flooded with warmth; and three, arms up, and the neck, yes, and more; the warmth grows, and on and on, and I laugh inside, deep inside. And four, and five. I die laughing and dance *Blind Woman's Bluff.*

Shush

I die laughing every time you start to act silly when we're eating soup, Papa. It's your favorite trick, and you delight in Mama's anger as the liquid squirts out our noses. They were so eager to keep you quiet when you were little that they called you Shush, a sound that springs to life with index finger over the lips: sshhhh! Now you're a lion, king of the jungle, crouching menacingly behind the doors of our childhood. To the beach on our bicycles, to run, to swim far, far out with that nimble stroke that seems to take you all the way across to the opposite shore of the river. What a kaleidoscope of surprises you are, sitting in the garden playing the violin or drawing with India ink: figures of skinny, potbellied kids on dirt roads. Why the blank gaze in their dark eyes? And you also sketch neighboring houses, and recite Heine, and dance the tango, and read, always read. It's not hard for me to love you: you give me advice only when I ask for it, you're not quick-tempered like Mama, you don't forbid me anything. You're the ideal father. As the years pass you laugh less and write more: *Is Politics a Dirty Word?*, articles about ethics and aesthetics, and some autobiographical pages at my request. They come with a note:

> I regret that my life has not been more heroic or novelesque. I'm much closer to a character from Kafka than to one from Byron.

You overlook one detail. While Kafka had a deadening desk job with an insurance company, you get to work at home, without schedules, enjoying what some would call freedom.

I got a telegram saying that my son had been freed. I dreamed that on the way home he fell down and was run over by a bus, and then hit again by a car going in the opposite direction. That he was mangled and left to die. Every time I tried to pull him off the road a car would speed by. And I thought, "My son was killed tonight." I looked at that telegram with his whole name on it, as if it were a gravestone.

They call out my whole name, first and last. The guy who takes me by the arm is kinder than he was before: I'm now a respectable blind person. He sits me down in front of a desk, across from a military officer who enunciates deliberately and with authority.

"It seems we made a mistake with you. But if you don't want any further complications, you'd better remember one thing: you were never here. Understand? We wouldn't want to feel obliged to proceed more harshly. So get this: nothing happened.

"Nothing escapes us: we know your family history, everything about your cousin and his girlfriend, each move of your uncle the journalist, what your cousins, the guerrillas, are up to. They could all suffer from any slip on your part. But if you behave and don't say anything you shouldn't, there won't be any problem."

Abel and Hugo

There were no problems between us, but I stopped seeing my cousins because of family quarrels: the older generation had a falling-out, and we no longer got together for New Year's or for birthdays. Still, their names popped up occasionally during dinner conversations.

"Did you know that Hugo finished medical school? He's working at the children's hospital."

"And Abelito?"

"He's about to graduate from high school, though he's only fourteen. I've heard that he's really tall and good-looking. They're going to help their father at the clinic. They're good kids, both of them."

"The boys showed up at the clinic one afternoon," my uncle tells me.

Abel was with me, and I heard my son Hugo rush up the stairs just as the shooting started. It was a trap. Armed men were pouring in from every corner, heading for the stairs to pursue Hugo on the rooftops. Abelito tried to block their way, and they grabbed him. They were yelling, kicking, throwing things around, spraying the place with bullets. They came back carrying Hugo's body; he seemed to have fainted. He wasn't wounded, and I realized that he'd poisoned himself. The famous cyanide pill. They asked me to give him artificial respiration, but there was nothing to be done. They took them both away, one alive and one dead.

I became fixated on this scene, trapped in it as in a tomb. I began to see policemen everywhere. I covered the cracks in my room with masking tape so they couldn't spy on me. One day an ambulance came and took me away. They gave me electroshock therapy. They declared me cured, but I'm a vegetable—or worse, a stone.

CASE 459. It has not been proven that on 19 April 1977 Abel Omar Strejilevich was arrested at the clinic of his father, Pedro Strejilevich, in Buenos Aires by security forces acting under the operational command of the First Army Corps. In fact, the writ of habeas corpus filed by his father before the local magistrate . . . does not indicate the manner in which the alleged disappeared was deprived of his freedom. Only a date is given, without naming witnesses or providing any further details that would help clarify the situation. There is mention of the previous disappearance of a brother of his, whose body was later found buried in an unmarked grave at La Chacarita Cemetery.

It must be added that the report presented by CONADEP also lacks specific details about this incident. There is only a reference made to a female cousin who reported his arrest.

These isolated elements can in no way serve as bona fide proof of such an event. There are no witnesses to his arrest nor any reports of his being seen at underground detention camps where others were illegally held.

CASE 460 [Hugo Strejilevich]. This court, having considered the evidence as presented by the counsel for the state and his request for absolution of the accused, does so rule in their favor.—*La sentencia*

At about that time Abel, my husband, Hugo, and I were staying at Pedro's clinic.

One afternoon when I arrive at the building during regular working hours I notice two motorcycles parked right in front and that the door is half-closed. I sense something odd. I start up the stairs and almost bump into this huge, dark-skinned goon. That's it for us, I think, it's all over. They'd made all the employees go outside except for a large woman who was still at her desk. They ask who I'm looking for, and I mention the doctor. Then a little guy wearing a Prince of Wales suit, which was fashionable at that time, comes in, gun in hand. I notice the ripped-out phone at his feet. I insist: "I'm looking for the doctor." "Which doctor?" "Dr. Pedro," I blurt out. "No, no, no, not in here, check the front room," he yells at me. As I'm going, I overhear a voice saying: "We have two packages, a white one and another one." Hugo and Abel, I think with a shudder. To think that all that happened in a few seconds! It seemed I'd been in there for an eternity, but it was actually less than a minute. Suddenly I see the large woman, and I open my eyes wide so that she'll catch my meaning. "My X-rays," I say. "They're not ready yet," she answers, staring hard. Just then a tall, blond guy steps in. I pretend to be angry and start to leave. "Still not ready? That's incredible. Fine, I'll check back tomorrow." I walk down the stairs. But when I get to the corner, I turn and run. I lose my documents, I lose everything as I run. I'm running as hard as I can, with no idea where to. I stop at a pay phone and, obviously in total denial of what I'd just seen, call Hugo to leave him a message. But they hear it and figure out who I am. So they go to my house and take a lot of my things: childhood pictures, college notebooks, a bag full of stuff. They take it all.

They take us, dragging our chains, out to the courtyard of what might be a police station—out of this hellhole, anyway. They press their guns to our necks: "On your feet, hands against the wall! Over here, you faggot, stand where I tell you!" They frisk us for weapons, as if we could be hiding anything. We are the chosen. If they bother to give us so many instructions, it must be that they intend to set us free. But you never know. They could just as easily finish us off with a couple of shots and pump the rest of the clip into us as well, for good measure.

Abel is shot because as they reach the sidewalk he bolts toward the corner. They shoot him in the leg and drag him away. Some witnesses tell me about it later. The goons wait until that evening, around eight o'clock—it was afternoon when they broke in—to take Hugo's body away. They must have thought they had stumbled upon a strategic hideout. But they were wrong. They didn't find a single weapon.

Let it be

Anonymous hands frisk us looking for weapons, while my own hands sift through the sheets of my memory to awaken the absent ones from among the folds. There they are: my friends, rowdy as usual, with a *zamba* between their fingers and the moon, leaning on their nostalgia. Songs right alongside utopias born of rage. Names are of no consequence; they're all alike. The ones shackled here are all alike too. We're all alike. We were a riot of laughter, not this silence frozen into a terminal shape. The lucidity of pain affords me the vain pride of not letting go when our names are about to crumble at the edge of dawn. We have grown used to farewells but not to this blind ceremony of leave-taking.

Unceremoniously we are shoved into a van. Let it be. Once and for all. I push my blindfold up slightly to spy where the first one gets dropped off. An empty lot, seemingly on the outskirts of the city. No houses or buildings in sight.

Next one. "Move it," they yell. He doesn't understand the command. Perhaps he thinks he's in front of a firing squad. He takes a few steps back. "Don't try to get smart, asshole." He walks a few steps forward. Still blind, lost.

"Start walking, you moron! Or do you want to stay with us forever?" He's paralyzed by doubt. Or by fear. "Gimme that gun and I'll blow him away for being such a jerk!"

Another voice intercedes: "Hurry it up, man, we have more cargo to dump off! You, count to a hundred and then take off the blindfold. If you do it before then, you're dead meat. You hear me?"

The van roars away.

"Turk here, over!"

"Brigade 315 headquarters. Positive."

"Do you know about GT2?"

"Affirmative. Stop by Logistics."

"Then look out for a three nine, over."

They stop once more. One, two, three. I'm number four. Alone with them.

JULIÁN THE TURK, Shortlife and Gonzalito, Sami the Crazy Seal, Red, the Colonel, Don Juan, Colors, the Soldier, Corky, Scorpion, Trigger-Happy, Wheaties, Blood, the German, Kung Fu, Old Cat, Birdie, Mouse, Turtle, Ant, Pepe Dirtbag, Doctor K, the Russian, the Jap, Fat King, Ramrod, Knee, Sling, the Hick, Deadbolt, Sparky, Jackal, Little Angel, Carnation, Father . . .

Finally it's my turn. The door opens and the street rescues me. The howl of the engine trails off, and I start counting out loud, gulping in breaths of fresh air. I follow the instructions scrupulously, as if they guaranteed salvation. Ninety-eight, ninety-nine, one hun-dred.

I was counting. I counted one, two, three, and very slowly up to sixty, to form a minute with the seconds, trying to help time pass, but it wouldn't.

While I count to a hundred they speed away. I can't hold out any longer and yank off my blindfold. The mercury lights blind me. I open my eyes little by little, giving them time to retrieve the notion of street lamps.

Some notions simply are lost—the notion of speed, the notion of distance, physical things like that. But they come back in a flash. It's like the first time you get up from a sickbed: it takes a little adjusting.

I adjust instantly to the layout of the place—winding roads, cobblestones, over there Caminito and the river. Yes, it's La Boca.

La Boca. Your barrio, Gabriel, the one you offered me when you were fifteen. The one we forged together, lingering on every corner, peeking into courtyards, investigating balconies and porches. We strolled there on Sundays, after the stores closed and we could have it all to ourselves—the sidewalks, the embankments, the small side streets, all bare like the autumn. La Boca, where the poor lose their treasures to floods; where the abandoned railroad tracks are haunted by old romantic tunes; where, frozen in time in the hallways of a playhouse, our theater of shadows lives on. La Boca, where balconies hide a thousand shadows.

BALCONIES HIDE / whispers and shadows / unseen pulsings / throb in doorways. / Three messages slice the streets / Forbidden. / Will die. / From now on. / Clocks are set / peepholes spy / angles tremble. / Solemn and armed / blood-stained honors march by / while in secret / and fleeting encounters / shy corners / speak out.

From the corner I observe the taverns of La Boca, where life is sprinkled with red wine until all hours. I step into the nearest one. I spy on the patrons of the night celebrating something with food, music, and noise aplenty. They are all having a good time, and laughter reverberates among pictures of flooded streets and posters of Carlos Gardel, guitars, and accordions. I ask to use the telephone; I don't want to waste any more time. I dial the number. A drowsy voice is startled:

"Norita!"

"Yes, it's me. I'm OK. I'm coming home."

I leave you no time to reply. I'm afraid they're following, listening to my every word. I'm afraid they'll take me in again. I go back out into the street with your voice echoing in my ears.

My first day out of jail I got up at dawn and stepped outside very early to see my first sunrise in nine years. I took a walk, wet my feet on the dew-covered grass, meandered along the train tracks, whatever—simply to experience that thing called freedom. That night, I remember, I went out for an ice cream. The lights made my head spin.

My head is spinning. I don't have any documents and not a single penny. I tell the waiter I was mugged and ask him for some change. I run to the bus stop clutching the coins in my hand. I'm fleeing, unused to being free.

I got used to being free in no time. Whenever I thought of being released I imagined it would be kind of weird, that I'd stumble on the sidewalk, feel totally disoriented. But no, it wasn't that way at all. I went out and felt great joy in simply walking down the street.

Walking down the street in the dark is not so easy. Careful: the path winds its way down some steps. I can't see a thing. Luckily I'm familiar with the area. I wait for the bus by the river, a black-and-white blur at this hour, on the cobblestone street. The stones speak of hands, of prisoners from another time. The Number 164 comes to a stop and turns off the engine. On this planet the only numbered thing is public transportation—how wonderful. I get on and pay the fare.

"We won't be leaving till a quarter to."

"What time is it now?"

"Two-thirty."

I have the whole bus to myself. I'm the only passenger. I choose the seat up front, all the better to see. And I can actually see quite clearly, despite my nearsightedness: a patrol car is parked right in front.

It used to be that patrol cars were really ancient, beat-up models, not even all the same make. Some Fords, some Chevrolets. I remember that we could always tell when one was approaching by all the rattling. They even used some bicycles to patrol. But they gradually upgraded when policemen turned into vigilantes, like our cops today.

Documents

All I need now is for that cop to climb up the two steps and board the bus. No sooner said than done. Now all I need is for him to come over to the only passenger: me.

"Documents."

One guy held my identity card up in the air in one hand, while he pulled off his pants with the other. He was about to tear the card up when someone told him not to. He said to me, "If you don't want me to tear it up, get on it," as he started ripping it up little by little. At that time you were nothing without proper identification. Sometimes people went to renew their documents and never came out again. Not having documents terrified me.

"Don't have any," I answer offhandedly, like someone reading from a not very original script.

"Don't you know it's forbidden to be without them?" he says in turn, as if rehearsing for opening night. They're all obsessed with documents.

I'm still obsessed with documents. Earlier this year, when I lost mine, I had to go to the police station to report it. So I'm sent to an officer who's fiddling with his computer and pays absolutely no attention to me. "All right," he says at long last. "You want to report it? Fine, let's do it, but you have to pay." At that exact moment I flash back to the scene of the guy slowly ripping up my identification. I want to leave and start to back out. Memories flood over me, and I'm reliving, reliving, reliving everything. All I manage to utter is, "No, no."

I stick to the script and reply: "Yes sir, I know I should carry my identification."

Finally he makes his pronouncement, those infallible last words: "Come with me."

Come with me

Two pairs of arms pull me out of the single file waiting at the border with Brazil. It's 1976 and I'm on my way home from vacation, brimming with sunlight and sand, with Copacabana and Sugarloaf. I don't pick up on the fact that the world spins 180 degrees toward darkness when we cross into Argentina. When I realize it, it's already too late. Alert, leery hands scrutinize my identity, pry into my most intimate recesses, search, find, and prepare to convict me if everything isn't in order. "This is subversive stuff!" the border guard shouts at me. It's drawings of Nazi concentration camps. Papa had sketched a realistic landscape of helmets and silhouettes of soldiers next to a barbed-wire fence against a backdrop of snow and smoke. On a corner the control tower, where a pair of armed guards stand watch.

"But, sir, look at the date: 1944!"

"Don't talk back to me, girl, and be glad I'm in a good mood today."

He pokes at my bones with his ballpoint pen. He crosses out my brain. He questions me about my activities, professional and otherwise. He catalogs me in his files and is ready to pronounce me guilty at the slightest slipup. He inspects my bag, leafs through the magazines, strips me naked with each turn of a page. He wrings me limp and dry, leaving me without a drop of innocence. He opens an envelope and holds the letter up to the sunlight.

"There's something written between the lines."

"It's the impressions from my own writing on another page."

"Answer only when I ask you!"

Next he turns his attention to a package. It's the only gift I'm bringing back. A wall clock. I watch him walk away with it and throw it down in the middle of a vacant lot. It does not explode. He comes back empty-handed.

"You can go. But take my advice and stop lugging around suspicious-looking parcels or you're going to end up at the station."

More information

At the station. I warned you, I warned you not to get your hopes up. I'm not afraid, not even disappointed. I didn't really expect anything better. Maybe they're testing me, checking to see if I've got a loose tongue. I'm bruised, penniless and without documents, wearing just a short-sleeved blouse in the dead of winter, at this time of night. All this apparently isn't considered unusual by those in charge of maintaining order. You have to play along, pretend everything's normal.

"Why aren't you carrying your ID?"

"I was mugged."

"Do you want to report the theft?"

"No sir, it's not worth it."

"What's your phone number?" I give it to him.

"Good evening, señora. We have a young lady here, at the police station, who claims to live at your address. We're calling to confirm that you know her and find out where she went tonight."

"Would you care to give us more information?"

THE FOLLOWING information comes from Juan de Luca, citizen of Argentina, married, Federal Police Inspector, given before the court where the case of the Athletic Club is being heard:

That the place was used exclusively for administrative functions appropriate to the Warehouse Division of the Federal Police force. That the warehouse occupied the ground floor, the first floor, and the terrace level of the building in question. Asked by His Honor to state whether the building had a basement, he answered: "No." That it had only a ground floor that served as a garage and a stairwell leading to the first floor, where uniforms were distributed to authorized personnel. Asked by H.H. to state whether detainees were ever held or transferred there, he answered: "No." Asked by H.H. to state whether at that time this division was under the control of the armed forces, he answered no, that what was under its control was the Federal Police unit, but not the Warehouse Division, since its functions had no relation to the operations carried out by the armed forces. . . . Asked by H.H. to state whether in this area there had ever been any official site with military or police personnel, he answered no, that he could not recall the existence of any. . . . Asked by H.H. whether he had anything else he wanted to add, he answered no, that he had nothing more to add. With that the session was concluded.—Athletic Club case, Center for Legal and Social Studies

Will this session ever end? The police station clock strikes 5:00 A.M. I've been here for two hours, and nothing happens. I want it to be over so I can run out.

Finally they drive me home in a patrol car—what a nice gesture on their part. On the way they try to talk with me.

It was obvious I was going to start talking the moment I got out. And that's just what I did. I talked and talked and have kept on talking nonstop right up till today. I went to the United Nations, I went to the Vatican, I went to the United States and to Spain—I went everywhere giving my testimony. I told them how a country lost somewhere in Latin America was strewn with concentration camps. I had gotten out, but there were many people going through what I had wanted to end every day. Even if it meant death. There were still people suffering that way. That's what I wished someone would do for me when I was inside. That's why I never stopped wanting to talk.

I don't feel like talking. I don't know what I could talk about with three policemen. I don't answer. At the door of my house two pairs of arms lift me up. I smile, feeling safe, and flutter endlessly like the butterfly on my globe lamp.

Business as usual

All aflutter they build me a water nest, and I sink into the warmth of the bathtub and of their words. Mama stays right by me and notices the scars that will not be sponged off. I remember the feel of her hands on the welts on my skin. My skin is the only thing that has changed during this time.

Otherwise it's business as usual: my bed still in its place, my globe lamp. My Vietnam poster, though, is missing. They must have shredded it. My volume of *Treasury for the Young* must not have caught their fancy, too bulky perhaps. My photo albums, notebooks, ponchos, clock, radio—those things also did not survive. Luckily they did not rip out the door, or the toilet, or make off with the furniture. No, just my diaries, my letters, small stuff like that. They acted soberly: an Army truck did not come and haul away everything in sight.

They had hauled away a lot of things: when I tried to dress I remembered that my clothes were packed. I opened the suitcase, but there was barely anything left in it. I put on a dressy blouse, the only thing I found. They'd taken whatever they could—just about everything except the refrigerator. And they came back for that the next day.

They can come back; they can always come back. They like you to live in apprehension of their possible return. Apprehensive and afraid, that's the way you should be. Sounds and voices filter into my dreams. Sleepless eyes have kept track of my every move from across the street ever since that afternoon in 1977.

Parallel stories about an afternoon in 1977 are told in *Rebeldía y esperanza* (Rebellion and hope) and in *A Single, Numberless Death*. The Argentine student returned home to 2900 Corrientes Street.

THE DOORMAN called her aside and told her that at noon several policemen in civilian clothes had been there asking about her.

What could they have told the doorman? He had to let them in.

THE YOUNG WOMAN—she was twenty-six—was surprised.

We were surprised.

AT 10:00 P.M. there was a knock on the door. The scene was the same one endured by thousands of people during the years of Videla-Massera-Martínez de Hoz. They pushed her to the floor, beat her, and questioned her about information they'd received.

The poor young Englishwoman, alone with the heroes of the fatherland. At least at home there were three of us.

THEY TOOK HER to a place about twenty minutes away that Diana would later recognize as the headquarters of the First Army Corps.

Twenty minutes to the north, fifteen or twenty to the south: routes to the same periphery, outside the boundaries of the official map. Were they comparing our answers, Gerardo?

THERE THEY interrogated her once more. Her answers were compared with those of Elizabeth Kaserman, being tortured in the next room. At dawn she is taken back to her apartment.

At dawn they take us back to our apartment.

THREE STAYED. They told her they were going to set a trap. Whoever knocked on the door would be hauled off to jail.

Would my friends be taken if I stayed?

WHEN THEY WERE READY one said, "Take off your clothes!"

We took them off, Diana. And right then a new battle began. The Dirty War.

THE TERRIFIED young woman, her eyes covered, was conscientiously raped by each one of them. Two hours apiece. While two slept the third one raped her. Anything went. A real victory of Argentine pricks over a helpless Englishwoman. Finally a victory! The goals add up. Argentina! Argentina! When they got hungry, they went down for pizza and Cokes. And back upstairs for more.

Did they eat a sandwich and drink a 7 UP after dumping me in my cell?

AT THE PEAK of her humiliation the theology student asked one of her rapists, "Are you Christians?" The rapist silently took the hand of the blindfolded girl, put it on his hairy chest, and made her touch a cross hanging from a chain. "We're Catholic," came the laconic reply.

Catholics who hate Catholics with foreign and divisive ideas, and Jews (always subversive elements), and Muslims, and Buddhists, not to mention atheists, all of them foreign sympathizers and traitors.

THE HAZING episode lasted three days and three nights. "If you say a word, you're history," she was told.

We're history, Diana.

AND THEN THEY LEFT. With everything—the appliances, the Latin American record collection, the jewelry, the money, the clothes.

Photos and ponchos, clocks, knickknacks, and coin collections.

WHATEVER they couldn't take was destroyed. They even ripped out the inner doors of the house.

Glass. They broke all the glass. The stained-glass windows.

TRIUMPH, TERROR, booty, and ravaged land. Dirty War. Ten days later Diana was able to leave the country.

We were able, Diana.

Buenos Aires, 7 April 1979

Dear daughter,

I read your letters over and over. I keep going back to them, until everything is etched in my mind in minute detail. Everything. How to multiply the images? By adding yours to mine, seeing you again, as on a screen, leaving your country with your little bundles.

Argentina is just an outline, a blur below the clouds, a dreamscape.

II

Until one day
they returned my name
and I went out into the halls of the world
to show it off.
I found masks
countries   slumbering profiles
tongues eager for novelties
absurd.

So I let myself walk
toward my nowhere
toward my nothingness
through gorges of footprints
without dew
not able to translate
my scars.

This name is not mine!
Mine
was a hundred   a thousand   it was all
mine
was body   was womb   was voice
it had neighbors   it whistled
it was for day   and for night
it was a god.

I have lost my name!
Along routes on a map
without corners   I screamed
among doors riddled with fear.

I want my name!
my proper name   curved   throbbing
I want it back!
wrapped in spring
with the r of row, row, row your boat
with the s of sugar and spice
with the t of twinkle, twinkle.

Not a dream

Today, in a dream, I saw a world adrift. There were figures flying or swimming around in space, enormous and tiny women, men in all sizes who doubled, tripled, multiplied. In the process bodies were created, bodies that seemed to be dancing with someone. That someone was a dress held up by the void of an absence. The couples played games of symmetry and surprise, appearing and disappearing against a black background that sprouted astonishment. A shimmering train crossed the horizon, going nowhere. A ship traversed the ocean in the opposite direction, but giant waves lashed the prow, covering it with foam, and the ship changed course. Airplane wings flew ceaselessly over the horizon, over the ocean, over any and all shores. I heard applause, but there was no one, only echoes. In the dream, I ran out of the dream.

It was not a dream. There seemed to be no one around when they plucked her from the bus and shoved her into a car. Same old story. In broad daylight, in the middle of downtown, in the bloom of her youth. Only that, in Olga's case, the one they wanted to pluck from the bus was me. How come? They'd already done it once! Right, and they could do it as often as they deemed necessary.

In '78 they kidnapped me for a few hours.

A cousin I never met shows my parents a photo ID from her teens. In black and white we are identical, almost. The Ford

Falcon without license plates starts driving around with Olga. In the middle of downtown, in broad daylight, a girl in full bloom doesn't understand what's going on; all she does is study and go to dances, no politics. Why, how, in a strange car, blindfolded, an anonymous voice on the walkie-talkie reciting her identifying characteristics: blond, blue eyes. Her hair gets tangled around powerful fingers: they're trying to yank off her dark wig, but they can't lift it from her scalp. The difference in color annoys them: "It's a dye job, you slut!"

1978. "We Argentinians are human, and we are also right," is the country's answer to human-rights violations. Now they're human and they're right. They no longer nab just anybody since there are far too many inquisitive foreigners coming to sniff out the state of our internal affairs. The hit men have no idea what to do with the package, so they drive it around town. Let the walkie-talkie decide whether or not to dump it.

The one who made the dumping decisions was a colonel who always stopped in to see me. In our exchanges I detected a weakness in him. I realized, first, that he was single. And second, that he had an oedipal fixation on his mother. He came around once every three months or so, and after each supervisory visit he gave some release orders.

So I work up a whole conversation based on my intuitions. The next time he comes into my cell I tell him, "You know, the one I really miss is my mother." I make no mention of wife, friends, or anyone else. I had put together a ton of stories from my life related to this theme. I go on: "All during my childhood and adolescence I studied just so I could get a degree and present it to my mother." One can expect a male chauvinist pig, an oedipal one to boot, to be touched by such words.

When the conversation is over he says to me, "I can't promise anything, but it could be that next time I might have some good news for you." And he asks, "Who do you associate with out in the courtyard?" I know I better tell the truth this time. So I do.

Later, when the list of those being released is posted, my name is there, along with those of all my courtyard buddies!

Time never runs out. But we do.—Gerardo Strejilevich

"I heard your voice before we were brought to the courtyard," one of Gerardo's friends tells me. We ran into each other at a march for human rights, and our voices were entwined for the rest of the night.

We were released at the same time, I'm sure. I recognized your voice. Didn't you ask for permission to move? What an idea! When they gave it to you, I got up the nerve and I started to move too, just slightly, nothing too noticeable. I kept listening to the voices to check whether Gerardo was there. We were kidnapped at the same time.

I kept quiet about Gerardo's disappearance out of fear. A fear that erupted first in nightly vomiting episodes and nightmares, and then in fear of those very nightmares. Your brother was also afraid—that's why he was spending the night at my house. I told him it was safer to sleep on a bus, on the ride over and back to La Plata or Rosario, for example. But that made him even more afraid. He didn't want to be alone. We walked over to my house, and he felt safer there.

"Open the door, brat!" they yelled, as if they really needed to be let in. Your brother was asleep in another room and wasn't going to have time to escape. I stalled, pretending not to remember where I'd put the key, which was right in the lock. Then I realized that Gerardo didn't know the house well enough to escape, and I opened the door.

It's not every day that you open the door and four rooms are ripped apart by a cyclone that shatters the past and yanks the hands off the clock. It's not every day that you try to escape and the clock has moved, the door is unhinged, the window stuck, and cornered you cry through minutes that do not tick away. The seconds that might have saved you have disappeared. It's not every day that you stumble and fall with hands behind your back, trapped in a night that tosses about the shreds of daily life. Dizzy, you whirl in a vortex of scraps, of yesterdays and nows crushed by orders and decrees. You get lost amid chairs overturned, drawers emptied, suitcases torn open, colors blanched out, maps slashed, roads severed. You barely make out the echoes reverberating, no longer in code—"You thought you could escape, bastard!"—as an enormous mouth devours you. Was it that way, Gerardo?

We're both pushed to the floor and against the wall so they can hit us. We're taken to a car and driven downtown. In about twenty minutes we arrive at the hellhole. And there we're separated.

You've become separated from your old self, Papa. You're worn out from playing Superman, from the arduous task of always being reasonable, even-keeled. The king of the jungle, weary of his role, has gone into hiding. He's resigned himself, given up hope; it's one way to get around despair without having to face it head on. When the pain is most intense the thread of anguish is severed, and a total calm similar to indifference sets in. The king of the jungle may appear composed. It's not serenity, though, but rather a grief that crushes his will. You've closed the shutters of your existence in order to avoid getting used to living with the absence. You don't even want to hear what I found out about Gerardo. "He's dead, that's all," you say, cutting me off. You want no more details.

. . . *THE DETAILS.* They're the first things that come to mind, the first things one has to forget. They are what seems unbearable, what appears to define the difference. *The details.*—Kaufman, *Heidegger y los judíos*

Since you want more details: Later I see him in the lion's den, a place where they keep us caged like animals, as the name indicates. They leave us together for a while. I'm not sure whether they want to eavesdrop on us or whether it's simply an oversight. We lower our blindfolds slightly and exchange a few words: that he'd said nothing about me, that I hadn't mentioned his name. But he tells me that he had talked. You know that Jews got the whole treatment. Then some guards realize we know each other and take him away.

In Jerusalem

Please take me away from this 115° in the shade: it's my one, feverish, ardent, hopeless wish. There's no cold water, only a few small glasses with tepid coffee-colored swill. Have some. "*Todah.* Thank you," I say. After the first sip I dissolve into cascades of sweat. "*L'chaim,*" he says. "To your health." The man continues searching through the sand, scrutinizing the grains as if rummaging in his grandmother's attic. His ancestors lived here, his sense of touch understands. Bedouins have no need to measure or study. They know what to do, where, how, when, and for what reason. We merely attempt to legally rob them of their knowledge.

They knead pita, that thin bread that smells like ashes. We open a few cans, clams and sardines packed in oil, our precarious wonders. They orient us in the labyrinth of stones and walls that emerge as we dig, with few tools but fingers aplenty. In the kingdom of hot, harsh winds, known as *khamsin,* sand is used to measure time, ownership of land is an insomniac's dream, and the dollar sign doesn't exist. We're lost despite, and because of, our instruments and our logic. The universe is this horizon of hazy dunes and a green oasis stretching up high toward the sun.

Exiled from myself

What really impressed me was the greenish artificial light that seemed to come from the ceiling. Always the same, night and day, since it couldn't be turned on or off. You got the feeling that you were somewhere outside of time, trapped in a never-changing place. A cell hidden from the world.

A cell hidden among the scent of pines and granite, which you call your lion's den. You hide your debatable identity in that house where the hours are measured in steps that come in and out, go up and down, come in once more. The impassive stairs carved into the rocks are visible from your window, and you spend your days staring blankly at them, between drags from a pipe stolen from your former self. I didn't have the pleasure of meeting that self. I know only the resurrected Andrés. The other one was left behind there, in La Plata, together with his identity card and his plans, the day a fleeting message smuggled out of jail set you in motion. You had to get lost. In Jerusalem you embody a character from your own stories, the one who hides in his room, behind a huge dust ball, to protect himself from the world. You withdraw inside your retreat, sitting on a wooden chair like Van Gogh's, but instead of approaching the window with brush in hand, you strain to gaze only inwardly, through some invisible peephole.

I seek you out one day at noon. This is not a courtesy call. I arrive the way I came into the world: to stay. Opening your door is like opening a book that intrigues you because of its anachronistic font and ragged edges, as if layers of time had stuck to its pages. A familiar voice addresses us from within your walls, demanding definitions. You're enacting the text of an Argentina that hasn't existed since 1976, already two years in the past. Your book is populated by bearded men with long hair given to existential defiance, engaged in coming to terms with, and assuming, their commitment.

I give you a lesson in commitment, plunking myself down right in the middle of your prose. Voices emerge from the walls, and we use them to cover up the din from the radio, the TV, the street.

> *THE WORLD IS A WALL; I'm not sure whether it's made of smooth, bare steel or of bare, smooth cement.*
>
> *Exile is like a child: once born, it continues to grow until death.*
>
> *Exile is a cow that can give poisoned milk.*
>
> *My time seems made up of only a few hours.*
>
> *I've arrived early at this exile from myself.*

Bombarded by another's language and culture, we play out our resistance to the siege, fighting in vain against the artillery of reality with phrases as our only weapons. We manage to lower the volume, but it's no use: the local sounds prevail, reminders that there's no place for us. Not here either. A couple of illiterate intellectuals, Andrés and Nora, unarmed soldiers on someone else's battlefield.

Did they do something?

You stay home in self-imposed exile, choosing not to travel to Israel with Mama. "Don't worry about me," you write, but even though you are a master at disguising your ostrich tendencies, we're aware that you're staying behind in order to avoid the world.

2 December 1978

My dears,

Allow me to inform you that I plan to have a roaring good time during your absence. I'll walk the southern suburbs, the better to admire their classic poverty, swim in the poisoned waters of the Río de la Plata, breathe in the barbecue-scented air of the Ezeiza woods, and greet the new year in the company of mosquitoes. Don't be jealous, your turn will come.

P.S. Did you do something about the physics book?

The book refers to Gerardo. Yes, yes. We spoke in the Knesset, the Israeli parliament. We knocked on doors. But there are certain puzzles that we're at a loss to resolve: if Israel sells weapons to Argentina, and if one of those weapons can be used to kill one of the disappeared, how many Israeli weapons are needed to kill thousands of disappeared?

In my opinion, thousands.

In my opinion, the establishment Jews were much too accommodating and soft-spoken. They did ask about prisoners, but in the case of the disappeared they inquired with a reserve that suited the military junta just fine. I remember an assembly at the AMIA, with community mothers in attendance, where we were told that we were being unfair, that they really were pressing for information about the disappeared. And one of the mothers told them, "This is a time to yell out loud, to make demands, not to act so cautiously, so obligingly, so reasonably."

Wisdom

Four pieces of wisdom lost, four molars gone—farewell to my youth. I'm obligingly waiting for the approval of the nurse, who parades by a row of victims eager for the ultimate blessing, the signal that guarantees safe-conduct out of this labyrinth of pain, gauze, and blood. Hundreds of aching mouths beg for mercy. I bear this final scene with meek indifference, tired of rebelling against rituals canonized by our society, such as tooth extractions.

Everything starts out fairly normally. A white lab coat approaches me flashing a Colgate smile.

"*Sliha giveret.* May I?"

Pleasantly surprised by the doctor's politeness, I place the bookmark on page four of Kafka's *The Trial* and obediently follow him to a chair that, by its mere presence, transforms me into a victim.

He asks me to open my mouth. I obey. Lower jaw down, head back, keep still. At that precise moment the nurse starts talking to him. I can't understand Hebrew, but I'm convinced that she rants on for at least two single-spaced pages. And my mouth is not hanging open out of astonishment.

Finally the doctor invades my intimate spaces with his clamps, picks, and expert glances. He's enthralled by my wisdom teeth, lovingly tended since early adolescence. He yanks out the first one. My mute body, spectator of its own agony, has no strength to react. The current of pain that penetrates to the roots of my gums at least diverts my thoughts away from the surgeon's face, from his distilled smile assuring me that we're almost there. Where, I wonder? "And there goes the second one!" A jabbing pain in the roof of my mouth confirms it.

The good thing is that one gets used to suffering, so I summon my courage. I'm prepared to pay in a lump sum, all four molars in one sitting. Just then the tormentor takes pity on me.

"*Maspik.* Enough for one day."

Chapter closed, my grumblings mere footnotes. There's no choice, not even in cases of elective pain. The nurse examines my mouth while hundreds of jaws in a row open and close, swallowing the administrative pardon. She's not to blame for the retroactive hatred I feel. I've been dragging it around since my involuntary internment in the infirmary at the Athletic Club, and sometimes my geographies get jumbled. I step out onto the street. On the sidewalk I sense the growing swelling of my cheek as the eyes of passersby strip me of my last remaining shreds of pride. I saunter past them with my disfigured face for all to see.

Here I come, ready or not

What ugly faces you make, Gerardo, standing before me in the bedroom: one hand pulls out a cheek, the other pushes up the nose, the tongue exits its cave and you holler the punishment:

Here I come, ready or not!

They're all hiding, Gerardo, all those who could've recognized you, and I lost. What's the point of going around with your picture—to show it to whom? Who could offer me one single gesture, one word, one new image of you? Who could cure me of this continual not-knowing that I drag through the calendar with me? Tossed into the ocean? Executed? Thrown into the river? Transferred to another location? Someone said you'd been moved to the Navy School of Mechanics, the ESMA. Could it be true? Each time I return to Argentina I try to fill the black holes of uncertainty by writing in a little notebook, as Mama used to do.

Why did I decide precisely today to sit down and pour my thoughts into this small, unfinished notebook, filled in part with algebra formulas that I never could, and never will, understand. Because it belonged to my son, and who knows when or if I'll see him again. Who knows if I'll still be here when he gets out, if he ever does. In any case, on this day, on which he entered his twenty-eighth year of life, if he's still among the living, I feel much too devastated to think of going out or even talking.

That's why I got out this notebook, which makes me feel close to him since it was his. If the day should come when I see him again, I'd like to tell him all this in person. If that's not to be, I'd at least like him to know how much we've missed him. I don't want to dwell on our anguish; he must have suffered infinitely more. And if at some point he was able to think, how he must have despaired thinking of our pain, since he was well aware that we had no idea what had happened to him. Perhaps we dream about him because he is concentrating so hard on us.

I know that he wouldn't want me to spend his birthday shut away inside these four walls, hurting. I hope he can forgive me for not being able to do what he would've liked. I cannot stop the succession of images, the regrets about our confrontations brought about by my outbursts.

Today is sunny and very warm, but I've closed the shutters and turned on the lamp. Daylight hurts. If it had only been overcast! But no, there's no choice.

Where are you? Do you know that you were born twenty-seven years ago today? Are you even aware of dates? What thoughts, memories, images might be crossing your mind right now? Did you look back on your existence before you ceased to belong to the world of the living, of those who come and go not thinking that it can all end, that something can just happen and then we are no more?

It's horrible not to know what happened to a person, especially one so dearly loved. That's the worst thing, far worse than death. In death there is at least certainty. All we have is an ever-present doubt that allows no respite and no peace. We go through the motions, living, talking, eating, walking, but we're not here. We're empty of the knowledge of what went on, and we long for the presence of that one special being. His things are here, his books, his writings, his clothes, but he is not.

Only someone who has gone through this can fathom what it's like. It's beyond imagination. At times the emptiness is such that I don't know how I get through the day having done things, walked down streets, chatted with people, leading what might seem a normal life. All that is on the outside; inside is the void. How can this be cured? Only with your return. And when might that be? There's no answer.

It's overwhelming to realize that we're just faceless numbers, that individuals simply don't matter. A person disappears, his or her place is filled by someone else, and life goes on. I hope this situation doesn't last too much longer. It will kill a lot of parents.

All-purpose lots

After thousands were killed there, the land around the Navy School of Mechanics was turned into a sports field. There's no limit to national plastic surgery, nor to the curiosity of a foreign correspondent, especially when coupled with my own. Kerrie, who works for a Canadian radio station, has asked for my help in preparing a program devoted to the Mothers of the Plaza de Mayo.

Today the plan is to interview the students from private schools who are playing ball on these very fields: all-purpose lots that twenty years ago housed torture chambers. We'd like to find out how these youngsters feel as they attempt to score goals here amid the echoes of kids their own age who disappeared.

I was majoring in science, and your brother sometimes played soccer with our team on a field near the School of Architecture. That was when we usually saw each other. He was the goalie. He seemed such a sincere kind of guy, so open and unaffected, though a little naive. Reading the testimony in Never Again *about what happened to Gerardo gave me goose bumps. What a tragedy that he fell into the clutches of those people.*

Those people have the right to let whoever they want to play in their fields. And since this is now a democracy, we have the right to ask questions of anyone we please, inside or outside the ESMA.

THE DETENTION CAMP INSIDE the Navy Mechanics School began functioning during the run-up to the 1976 coup. . . . The camp functioned in the officers' club, a three-story building with a basement, and a huge attic. The officers slept on the first two floors; in the basement the torturers plied their trade; on the third floor and in the attic, the prisoners awaited their fate.—Andersen, *Dossier Secreto*

In order to find our way to the ESMA, we ask the few residents of the area for directions. They're mostly boys, playing ball in some surrounding barren fields.

"It's that way," they say, pointing, "across the bridge."

They hung her under the bridge, with this very rope. Look at this picture of my daughter, look at the blindfold over her eyes. This is a powerful piece of evidence that they cannot deny. I have her skirt right here, in this bag. It's in my possession. These pictures are going to be their undoing. And notice the ultimate humiliation, the sign that they put up after they hung her. "I was a Montonera." Can you imagine? They kept her there for an entire day, showing off her corpse under that sign. And people passed by the body, by that sign, and just kept on walking.

We walk around the building following a dirt path to avoid the guards. It eventually turns into a road that leads to the back of the ESMA. Out in those immense open spaces we're accompanied only by the sound of our own footsteps.

What police station?

I hear your muffled footsteps echoing in the stillness of the hallway. Faint footsteps, Papa, the kind that hesitate at the edge of the cliff, that stop just short of yielding to the seductive immensity slumbering below. Your voice defies modulation; it comes out sounding harsh, rusty.

"I went to the police station," you say with effort.

Hands clasped together are speaking, tense fingers searching through rubble.

"I told them that you'd already disappeared once in '77 and that I was very worried because you were late getting home tonight." Your voice now is just a thread, emanating either from your gut or from infinity.

"They opened a file with your name. They said they would close it when you came back. You have to go there."

Now the hands come apart and wave about as if clearing some space, making room to breathe.

How to embrace you, how to free you from that oppressive dread, the monster that crushes your lungs, renders you pathetic and helpless? How to do it if I too am gasping for air, my body crushed, deformed? With barely a fraction of my vocal chords I ask you to come with me. I must walk into a police station, throw myself into the jaws of that savage beast that hounds us. I cannot think. Stepping on those tiles, even if they're different ones, smelling that smell, even if it's different, listening to those voices, to that clicking of typewriters. It's all the same.

We go in together. Once inside, our eyes survey a one-dimensional, abstract plane. I feel nothing.

Guards at the entrance, flagstone courtyard, paint peeling off the walls. And the smell, that blue smell. The desk for confessions, explanations, numbers, and signatures. We both sign.

I've no idea which police station you're coming out of—short steps, arm bent so that I can cling to it. I leave my own police station in the wee hours of a winter morning. You leave the first one on a frigid July day, all alone, since no one goes with you to report the two kidnappings. You leave another station, where kerosene heaters don't succeed in taking the chill off the bureaucratic indifference. You leave yet one more, where noisy fans cannot cool the hardened indifference caked on the walls, on the skin of policemen taking down the same information over and over, knowing that you know that they know what they say they don't know.

The stations of habeas corpus: you bring papers in and come out with empty hands. I wish you could scream, but you are mute and stooping. An aching shadow hangs from your body, and I don't know how to ease the pain. That night, in the darkness, I put my arm through yours and we tell each other the silence.

The unexpected

"Silence hides the impossibility of saying the horrible, the unspeakable." Words leap off the printed page, fly out the window, and get plastered on the façade of a building from my past. It should come as no surprise—the extraordinary can stare at us from any opening. Chance, or rather the unexpected, materializes squarely before me, and it has the expected effect: I cannot believe it.

So many years of silence and still the same geographies, identical obsessions. The bus drives right by *my* police station. Fate or chance, same difference. I decide to get out. Half a block away the typical line of patrol cars. They're clunkers, at least fifteen years old. A car is backing into a parking space, and the brake lights take me back sixteen years, to that July night when they let me go: my cotton blouse, their winter uniforms, my empty pockets, their weapons. We got out of the car and entered through the main gate. Now, for the first time, I notice the façade: two murals by Quinquela Martín with imposing ships and scores of dockworkers. Quinquela didn't paint policemen. Over there a telephone where a hand must have dialed my number. The shape of my past.

The guard says nothing to this nosy lady peering into his place of work: terra-cotta tiles, light-colored walls, warm shades, primary tones. That night in July 1977 a call from the Athletic Club:

"We just dumped the goods."

Not a cowboy flick

"Look over there!"

Just like in the movies, at that precise moment an Army truck pulls up, right in front of our perfectly innocent noses. It's about to drive in. One of the heroines runs to ask, with her most appealing smile, if they can go in too. Lo and behold, open sesame.

Open the barriers / and let her in / open the door to the sun. Kerrie and Nora stand on the other side of the fence now, literally inside the ESMA, staring in astonishment as the man gets out of the truck to lock the gate. The barriers close.

"They open the mail and read it," Papa tells me.

That's why our letters are always in code. Gerardo is "the book."

"They even let you know they're doing it: after they read them, they stamp the seal of the Ministry of the Interior over the name of the sender, to leave no doubt as to who lords over intimacy in this country."

Official government letters, however, always arrive hermetically sealed.

10 July 1979

Dear Nora,

Official replies are written in such hermetic terms that one ends up looking elsewhere for any hint of encouragement. Do you believe in parapsychology? We sent a check to one of those psychics. He answered that the book still exists. We don't really believe this, although we cannot help but wonder. How do we get at the truth?

"The truth is that there's only one way out of here: through the main door," I say, as if physically measuring the remainder of our freedom.

"Don't worry; if we want out, we can climb over the gate."

"You're crazy! We don't climb over gates here! This isn't a cowboy flick, Kerrie. And besides, keep in mind that we'd need at least two horses!" As I say this I wonder if we aren't indeed in a film.

We used to go to the movies in the neighborhood, to see war movies or cowboy flicks. When the Seventh Cavalry arrived, instead of clapping there would be booing, and when the Indians showed up, we applauded. If they were showing World War II movies, we applauded the Nazis. Why? Because we only knew about the Nazis from what the Hollywood films showed: that they were warriors. They didn't show the repression. The Nazis were the bad guys, they had a uniform, and they were up against another set of uniforms. We were for the bad guys because we were anti-American.

What to do?

What should we do with all this? On her lapel, hidden under a scarf, the Argentine actress wears a microphone. The point: to record her feelings at the place where her brother presumably was taken. Feelings? Actors follow a script; they're not asked to improvise! I cannot think. Death is not a good conversation topic. Death dies. It is autumn. The sun touches the leaves of the elm tree, weighing them down. They fall, one by one, to the rhythm of yellow chirping.

THE DETENTION CAMP located at the ESMA . . . began operating as the March 1976 coup was being prepared. It went through many incarnations, under the supervision of various groups with different styles of repression. It was closed only in November 1983, days before the new constitutional government assumed power.

During those ninety-two months of genocidal furor an estimated 5,000 detained-disappeared passed through its gates. . . .

For this reason it holds the degrading distinction of being one of the main underground centers of torture and illegal imprisonment operated by the military dictatorship.—Paoletti, *Como los nazis, como en Vietnam*

I'm standing at the scene of the events, where life curdles into clumps of horror. The scene of the events—a refined expression for glossing over both the subject and the actions. I sift through the earth, searching for their faces. Thick mud, silhouettes, thousands of bodies diffused in the breeze.

We were bodies moving almost blindly through the night. It was pouring rain and the camp was dark, but we had orders to attack and capture the flag. This was part of our unit's military training. Those in the rear had to cover for us. I was among the attackers. After some fumbling about we broke in through the kitchen, with a loud crash. It was easy since there was only one guard; the others had all gone to sleep.
This was more like a rugby game than military training.

GOOOOOOAAAAALLLLL!

At the far end of the playing field, a soccer game. A fight to the death for the ball, bouncing from one foot to the other. There's nowhere, and no way, to glimpse the buried past. "GOOAALL!" reverberates across the grounds.

"THEY SAY that the athletic field is filled with the bodies of guerrillas, and that's wrong. It may be that the corpse of some wounded person who couldn't take it and died was cremated there."
"In what way?"
"They burned it. That's another topic that made the rounds. . . ."
"How many?"
"Very few."

"In other words, they were taken up in airplanes when they were capable of walking."

"They were always capable of walking. Those who were wounded were treated."

"But in the cases you mention, the wounded could not—"

"Not wounded, no. Dead. They arrived wounded. They were arrested and resisted arrest, and sometimes they didn't survive, like anyone wounded in a war."

"Was there some special place for this?"

"No, no. Behind. But these were very rare cases."

"Did they have special installations?"

"No, there was never anything out of the ordinary. What's more, the athletic field was always in use. It was never shut down."

"They burned a body and then played soccer on the athletic field?"

"Noooo. That athletic field is very big. It's on land reclaimed from the river. The farthest part is almost inaccessible; it's not in use. It's behind everything, next to the river."—Navy Captain Adolfo Scilingo interviewed by Horacio Verbitsky, 1995, in Verbitsky, *The Flight*

We head toward the back, close to the river. I hide behind a heavy American accent. Once again I stand before the cameras without a script.

"Don't you feel kind of weird playing here, in a place like this?"

I'm afraid they'll think we're aliens.

"What do you mean?"

Kerrie comes to my aid: "Well, they say that people were tortured here."

"Oh, I don't know about that. Nothing's really known for sure. If you want to ask, you can go over to that building and talk to the instructors."

"BUT LARRY, the ESMA is a school. Do you really believe that we tortured people there?"—Admiral Massera to *New York Times* journalist Larry Burns

FOR ONE THING, this building happens to be a school; for another, its name includes the word "mechanics." It's as if some buildings were predestined to fulfill a certain tragic function.—Horacio González

Ask the instructors! A bit late to change our minds. We cannot possibly retrace our steps, jump over the gate, go back to the path, rewind the video of this series that is definitely turning into a cowboy flick. Eyes wide open, senses on alert, and with a growing ball of fear rising from the pit of the stomach up to the mouth, blotting out the present moment and getting stuck between the throat and revulsion, we knock on the door.

"Come in."

Ghosts

"Come in," you say dryly.

You wouldn't even pick me up at the airport, even though you haven't seen me in three years. Time has left its mark on you, Papa. You seem unable to bridge the distance between these inner corridors and the plaza that, by forcing you into history, might save you from the void. Your hands, now so unsure of themselves that they don't dare emerge from your pockets, are helpless to give shape to your pain. Alone with your memories, you rehash that failure that you wear like a coat over your old age. You wander from room to room like someone inspecting an apartment for rent. You're taking your leave of life. "The world leaves us behind long before we depart forever," you like to say, perhaps as a warning. Obsessions gnaw away at you relentlessly. Hands behind your back, you roam around your fears, nodding your head, on the verge of spilling its bitter contents. You bear a heavy load. It takes you longer to walk across the hallway than it would take to recall your entire life.

We walk through the door of the building, to the surprise of an officer and an instructor enjoying a well-deserved rest. While they appear to be alone, the walls are inhabited by ghosts.

Ghosts are not entitled to receive any kind of reparation; this goes without saying, and it wouldn't occur to anyone to question it. What I do have reason to question is whether I really am one of those ghosts. Nevertheless, government forms seem to know more than I do in this and many other ways that are beyond me.

According to a new decree passed in the early nineties by the party then in office, former political prisoners can claim a certain amount of money for each day spent behind bars. That's fine for the ones who were given due process. But those of us in legal limbo, neither officially incarcerated nor held by legitimately recognized military forces, logically don't appear on any records. We, therefore, do not exist, and our existence is precisely what we're trying to prove.

Former prisoners can give depositions and fill out the appropriate forms at the Office of Human Rights. But the ex-disappeared have nowhere to give depositions and no forms to fill out. Like the disappeared, they do not exist.

APPLICATION FOR BENEFITS, DECREE 24.043

Place and date_____

TO THE NATIONAL COMMISSION ON HUMAN RIGHTS of the MINISTRY OF THE INTERIOR

The undersigned hereby requests the benefits established under Decree 24.043

BENEFICIARY:

Name:_____

IDENTIFICATION:

Type:_____ Number:_____

HOME ADDRESS:_____

City:_____ Province:_____ Postal Code:_____

CASE STATUS

    Commenced on _____

    Decree Number _____

    Ended on_____

    Decree Number _____

CASES OF CIVILIANS DETAINED BY MILITARY COURTS:

Date of arrest:_____ Place:_____

Date of release:_____

Acting court:_____

Evidence:_____

CASES OF ARREST PREVIOUS TO THE DECREE OR WITHOUT
JUDICIAL ORDERS:

Date of arrest:_____

Evidence:_____

SWORN STATEMENT: I hereby swear under oath that the information provided above is true and that I have not received any previous compensation in reference to the events encompassed under Decree 24.043.

Signature of the beneficiary or his/her representative:

_____

Notary Public_____

    I have to explain to the officer what we're doing at the ESMA. My fake foreign accent gets tangled on the wires of the tape recorder and I find myself tongue-tied.

My grandchildren became tongue-tied when we arrived in the
United States. It was a real circus. The children of our own disap-
peared children had been accepted at a school in New York. In or-
der for us as legal guardians to be able to enroll them, we had to
state that the children spoke English, even though they didn't. Not
a word. I arrived there with the three kids, and when they were
asked their name and age, they just froze. I was afraid we'd be sent
back home, so I told the immigration officer, "Well, they know the
basics of English . . . ," and he replied, "Yes, basics indeed, ma'am."
By this time everyone else had already left, and I was there alone
with the three kids wondering what to do.

I'm wondering what we'll do in this stage setting we've just
entered. At the rear, from behind an oak table that takes up half
the room, under windows so tall that they look out onto
nowhere, a civilian looks askance at us. There are banners on the
walls, a telephone, some padded chairs. The contrast between
the cozy aspect of the room and what I know about its history
stirs in me an irrepressible need to pee. While Kerrie is introduc-
ing herself, I ask to use the restroom. At the end of the hall, to
your left. A diminutive room with a dirty window and a toilet that,
luckily, is in working order.

Out of order
The toilet in the small bathroom is out of order.
The kitchen window is stuck: do not close.
The bathtub tiles are loose: do not lean on the edge.
The lock to the back door is broken: do not open.
The washing machine leaks: do not use.
Do not turn on several lights at once: fuses will blow.

Even before I have a chance to put down my luggage in Gerardo's room, my favorite, you hand me a meticulously handwrit-
ten sheet of paper. A summary of your new chapter of humanis-

tic philosophy, I assume, the by-product of long hours of reflection. I wasn't expecting such a welcome ceremony, Papa! I thank you before looking it over. I go to the window, open the shutters to let in some light, and read the list: a detailed picture of the anonymous and devastating deterioration that is encroaching on your present.

Have you forgotten that you're an architect? No, but the cracks in your world can no longer be repaired. Destruction rules and requires one to step with utmost care so as not to upset the precarious balance of the building. Balance? There are no joints or pillars, no columns for support. Your life floats suspended in an uncertainty that bumps against more and more doubts, against problems that grow exponentially, although not yet infinitely. It's more like a chain reaction that ends in an explosion. I grow weary suggesting concrete ways in which to solve every problem: sell the apartment, call the plumber, have duplicate keys made. There are no keys to fit your lock. But I still cannot see that this, precisely, is the problem. I lose my patience because you don't cooperate. My anguish is disguised as anger. I get angry at getting angry. I go out in search of scarecrows to frighten away my rage, leaving you alone.

I'm alone in the small bathroom, no cameras in sight. I'd like to flush the crappy microphone that I'm carrying down the toilet, but I settle for shoving it to the bottom of my pocketbook. I hide my ID card in my panties—what better place for safekeeping my identity?

You covered up your identity marks in order to protect yourself, and you never found them again. Mama's been gone for three years, and her absence is written all over you—forlorn as the desk, dim as the light in the hallway. You make an effort to smile, but your muscles don't respond. You take me on a tour of the rooms: the same old things are now burdened with a heavy layer of time. The effort it takes to sidestep the anguish puts me on edge.

I don't know what to do with my nerves when they snap as I return from the restroom and hear Kerrie's heavily accented Spanish:

"She's writing a book."

Never Again

Books help me to kill time and ease anxiety attacks, especially when I have to stand in line. At the office of the Commission on Human Rights I open up Juan José Saer's *Shoreless River.* The eyes of the bearded man waiting next to me linger on the title. Is he interested, perhaps? I'm about to explain that it refers to that deceitful body of water, the Río de la Plata, our supposedly sweet freshwater sea. It's a chronicle of that river, which turned out to be so bitter, populated by a cacophony of floating corpses. The chatter of three secretaries who munch on cookies to the rhythm of gossip prevails over my didactic zeal. Minutes stretch so thin that they're about to snap, until I finally ask my neighbor if any of those women are supposed to be helping the public. He answers that depositions are taken in an adjacent room and there's only one person assigned to the task. "But I'm not here to give a deposition; I just want to ask a question!" He urges me to clarify that; otherwise I risk wasting the whole afternoon here. A woman comes out, teary-eyed after telling her story. She's a former political prisoner taking the first steps toward claiming her reparation from the government.

I'm here merely to confirm that I don't show up on any of the lists of persons legally incarcerated and therefore fully authorized to file claims. As I near the head of the line, the secretary ushers me in along with the bearded man. Before sitting down, I explain my case and spell my last name. While the employee is checking his catalog of names, the bearded guy swings around and stares at me:

"Did your testimony appear in *Nunca Más?*"

I have never felt so dejectedly famous.

"Yes," I whisper, confounded by the question that invalidates the fertile proofs of my nonexistence. But my curiosity, more ingrained even than theological doubt, has been stirred:

"Have you read it?"

He swiftly deals his *coup de grâce:*

"I transcribed your testimony. Is your name Noemí?"

"Nora, but I think that Noemí appears on the same page. Amazing recall! Did you transcribe the whole thing?"

"No, just a few parts."

"What a coincidence!" I mumble, dumbstruck, as he reaches out to shake my hand.

I barely manage to take it, and look at him as if he were an old friend whom I scarcely recognize after light-years of absence. Giddy from the impact of abruptly finding such a fortuitous witness to corroborate my existence, I leave the office. As I'm about to close the enormous glass door, its panels covered with pennants and discolored curtains, I'm paralyzed by a very unmethodical doubt: Will my steps be audible as I exit?

Interrogation

I step firmly from the restroom to the main office, hoping to catch Kerrie's attention and cut short her speech. Her crusade for justice is unrelenting: the truth, the whole truth, nothing but the truth. And she's telling them about her radio program dealing with the Mothers of the Plaza de Mayo. I wish the earth would open up and swallow me whole! The officer makes a phone call and with deliberate slowness announces from under his thick protective mustache:

"They're coming to escort you back to the entrance."

They escorted you to the exit of the world, Gerardo, and didn't let me say good-bye to you. *Oh, you cannot reach me now, / Oh, no matter how you try, / good-bye cruel world, it's over / walk on by.* Did you perhaps exit with a song? Is it true that death is blue, that it is red, that it is silence?

We had such little time to be together, but being together is a manner of speaking. By definition a younger sister's life demands an older brother. I'm left without my basic premise, playing with your shorts-clad shadow behind the screen of longing. A mischievous-looking shadow, that sneers at everything. You laugh triumphantly even when you have knee surgery. But whatever for, if your asthma is already reason enough to keep you out of the draft?

Were they perhaps drafted, these little lead soldiers that come to get us?

"In-ter-ro-ga-tion," I whisper to Kerrie.

My cold blood saved me from several risky interrogation sessions. One time I was at a café on the corner of Corrientes and Boulogne sur Mer, preparing a report with some friends. There were five of us at the table, carrying weapons inside a bullet-proof briefcase that we used as a shield. Nothing else. Suddenly the cops burst in, a whole gang of them, and blocked both exit doors. The café was full, and they started checking the people closest to the doors, frisking them for weapons and looking over their identifications. Table after table, one by one. And we sat there, frozen, while the officers went around.

When one of them gets near to where we're sitting, I quip, "Hey, buddy, make sure you check these guys out real good, these are . . . they're into it up to their ears." The guy grins.

*They approach the table next to ours—"Your papers, please"—
they make the people stand up, frisk them. Then over to the next
one, and another, and yet one more after that. When they finish
with the last one, we mumble through our teeth, "Here they come
now." The officer walks right by, waves to us, and leaves.*

They never know

The officer leaves us in the hands of the recruits. Trying to get a
grip on myself, I focus my attention on their field uniforms. *Cata-
marca landscape / with its varied shades of green.*

Boots, caps, and particularly those rifles. We cross a bridge
and walk through an impeccable miniature city with stately
buildings and narrow cobblestone streets.

THE SPRAWLING complex in the residential Nuñez district in
northern Buenos Aires, far away from the salt spray of the high
seas, was the navy's most important political presence in the
capital. Its well-kept white buildings and brown wooden shutters reflected the navy men's self-image as a cut above, their su-
periority over their mongrel cousins in the army.—Andersen,
Dossier Secreto

"Bathurst," reads a sign. "Strange how the names weren't
changed after the Falklands War—or the Malvinas, as you call
them," notes Kerrie. She tries to make small talk with a soldier
who stares into space and aims his profile away from the voice.

They never know, never voice an opinion.

*The first rumblings about the Malvinas caused quite a stir.
Everybody wanted to enlist; in our cell block only two of us dis-
agreed. It seemed such a hare-brained scheme, yet practically
everyone was in favor of the war. I don't think even a tenth of the
people in prison had any notion that this was a real blunder, not
worth their lives. To top it off, they'd turn on the radio and the TV
in the corridor so that prisoners could hear the official newscasts:*

*journalists speaking passionately about how our country was win-
ning the war. This news brought about generalized euphoria.
Some went so far as to rally in support of General Galtieri! The two
of us were considered traitors: not only were we unwilling to fight
but we accused the government of being a pack of loonies, ready to
start a war that could never be won. Finally the day came when a
sign-up sheet was circulated. Many of the prisoners volunteered to
go. They never actually went, but they did offer. They got together
with the prison directors, even with a few military officers, to con-
vey to them their willingness to go to the front. Supporting Galtieri
was considered merely a minor contradiction, a problem internal
to Argentina. Great Britain was the imperialist power against which
we ought to rally as one. The whole country united against the
British. Until news of the defeat began to trickle in.*

Today is Wednesday too

Kerrie keeps on talking about the Malvinas, about the defeat,
about countless other topics. A masterful monologue. My adrena-
line pumps with a force directly proportional to the square of the
distance that we're traversing. Vanish, traces of doped-up bodies!

"HOW WERE THE unconscious people taken to the door?"
    "Between two men."
    "They were dragged?"
    "They were carried to the door."
    "They remained unconscious."
    "Totally unconscious. No one suffered in the least."
    "There was never any exception to that?"
    This question seems to disturb him more than the others.
He thinks and thinks again before answering.
    "No. None I can attest to." . . .
    "Was any study made to determine in what place. . . ?"
    "I'm sure there must have been some studies. I imagine
there were. Out on the open ocean."
    "How many people do you calculate were killed in this way?"
    "Between fifteen and twenty per Wednesday."

"For how long?"
"Two years."
"Two years, a hundred Wednesdays, from fifteen hundred to two thousand people."—Navy Captain Scilingo interviewed by Horacio Verbitsky

Today is Wednesday too. They make us walk outside for about ten minutes. It's winter: the pitiless cold races up from our feet to our shoulders and down again, back and forth, back and forth.

You pace back and forth in the room, Gerardo, as if trying to escape from yourself. This occurs to me only now, going over the scene in my mind. And I, like an idiot, glued to those endless philosophy books. I just didn't get it.

Plaid shirt, jeans, black belt. Hardly ever without that dark blue overcoat that wraps around you like a glove. If your coat doesn't protect you, what will? It makes me edgy to see you looking out the window, checking to see whether you're being followed.

"Why don't you just leave the country, Gerardo? The people from the Jewish agency can get you into Israel. That would help."

"Can't go to the airport without a marriage certificate. Remember, Graciela's a goy. Before we could emigrate to Israel we'd have to get married. And in order to get married we need time."

You didn't have time. That's why I take time to retrace the maybes of your footsteps.

The Costa Dorada

My own footsteps enter into dialogue with whitewashed buildings, cobblestone streets, lamps, porches, breakwaters, tiled roofs, and flower-filled balconies. I'm familiar with the entire vocabulary of tastes and smells, even though I've never set foot here before. We open the gate leading into Six Arches. The door to your new house in Catalonia, Andrés, closes a long gap—a gap opened by the yellow of your letters that I eagerly awaited during my frenzied, sleepless nights in Jerusalem. You skittered away from the Middle East as soon as you heard the word *army*. The Israeli passport had a price tag, a high one for a change of skin. Was that really you, that shocked face, with cropped hair minus beard and glasses? How did you resign yourself to this flat, rectangular reality? How did you get used to your signature in Hebrew? And to your name pronounced so harshly? After mulling over the matter, you gave it a Copernican twist: you showed up in an envelope stamped in another galaxy, gleeful on the mailbox's red tongue, announcing your move to Barcelona. The word *Spain* is the first motionless motor that cranks up a series of events. I pack in a flash. Now you live on the Costa Dorada. Every coast has its golden glow, and mine appears on the horizon, glimpsed through the window of the train: Sitges.

"Trains that pull onto platform number 2 continue to Sitges." Such strange words blaring from the loudspeakers.

"Platform? What are they talking about?"

"Listen, girl, we speak real Spanish here!"

Platform is the word they use for "quai." Just a slight tweak and my Spanish is on its way. And how it slips and glides tirelessly on the curves, the cliffs of language! In this country my tongue doesn't suffer from paralysis.

I don't know what language to use to tell them what I think, these four impeccably groomed *milicos* who have so cordially escorted us. As usual, they find the words before I do; as usual, they use the imperative, in any language.

"Wait here, señoras."

You'll have to wait

"But look here, señora," he said, "our hands are callused from taking so many of our own relatives' corpses to their graves." "Colonel," I answered, "your hands may be callused, but at least you have graves. The mothers' hands are callused too, but it's from filling out so many forms. We have no graves because you deprived us of them."

"You'll have to wait until you're called in," a uniformed Navy recruit informs us. I don't know how to break the silence that surrounds his words like a threat.

In prison we tried to break the silence, to generate contact with the others. Until then I'd no idea how to speak in code, but little by little you build up a vocabulary. We devised a very rudimentary way of talking with taps on the wall. To make a Z you had to tap thirty times! It would've been simpler to misspell some words and just use an S, don't you agree? Later on, one of the other prisoners told us to place our tin cup against the wall to amplify the sounds, like with a microphone. You can both speak and listen through it, so we could actually talk. In jail I also learned to communicate in Morse code, without words, in any way possible. The point was to overcome isolation, one of the most severe of the psychological problems that affected us. So we talked.

We talk to each other in English. Kerrie repeats that we're going to be thrown out any second. By definition, a Canadian citizen simply cannot understand the workings of the universe in the Southern Hemisphere. To her, this is like the far side of the moon: invisible.

Sitges

Coming from Israel, Spain is the far side of the moon. And just as one plants a flag on the moon, I plunk down my eighty pounds of portable home in your room in Sitges. I scatter books around, invade your medicine cabinet with pills to fight off germs and sorrow. I keep the window clear of clutter so that Mediterranean sunlight can flood walls and pictures. Despite all my good-luck charms, an oppressive weight bears down on me. I don't know what's wrong, just that my memory hurts. A chorus of voices demanding something rises like a tide. They speak in unison, screaming dissonant rhymes. One voice stands out, the interrogator's.

Telling the truth

"They're going to interrogate us," I mutter, "and our versions better agree." She's her logical self: let's tell the truth. Maybe she has a point. After all, we've committed no crime. But reason doesn't make a dent on sheer terror.

"Please, Kerrie, don't mention the Mothers again . . ."

The Mothers demonstrated right in front of the Navy School of Mechanics. Twenty of us marched by the building, yelling "Murderers!" and writing on the sidewalks: "Here people were locked up, tortured, killed." And we handed out leaflets to passengers in buses driving by, all of whom would open their eyes really wide. When the guys at the ESMA saw women with kerchief-covered heads approaching, they chuckled at first; then they didn't know what to do; then they sneered; then they got jumpy. Our yelling caught people's attention, and some kids coming out of school started to laugh at the commotion we were making, but then they came up close and stayed with us. They wanted to find out what it was all about. And we told them.

I think this is very important, so they won't be deceived by the official version of history. When they grow up, they'll say, "No, we saw those women, and we know they weren't crazy."

Since the ESMA has several different doors, we walked from one to the other, soldiers following on their side of the fence, weapons at the ready just in case. We were certain that nothing would happen, but still, just picture it: on the outside, old ladies clamoring for their children; on the inside, brave Navy recruits marking our every step. One of them got close to us from his side of the fence and called out: "What's going on? What's all the commotion about?" "Ah, you mean you don't know what happened here?" "Nooo . . . sure, there might have been some prisoners, but . . ." Then one of the Mothers, in a thoroughly guileless tone, offered: "Let me tell you what happened." And she started to explain about the torture, about the murders, about all the things we knew. She even mentioned a tank of water where they dunked prisoners. The guy listened with a smirk.

The smirking Navy officers don't trust us because we mumble to each other, because we avoided the main door, and because we came out of nowhere asking weird questions about a remote past that none of them can recall.

"THE DAY OF THE 'TRANSFER' everything was very tense. The detainees were beginning to be called by number," recalled several former prisoners at the Navy Mechanics School, a well-tended complex of white buildings sandwiched along the Río de la Plata between two of Buenos Aires' wealthiest neighborhoods. "They were taken to a nursing station in the basement, where a medical assistant was waiting to give them an injection that put them to sleep, but didn't kill them. Still alive, they were carried out and put into a truck, taken asleep to the municipal airport and loaded onto an airplane headed south, to the open sea, where they were thrown out alive.—Andersen, *Dossier Secreto*

They're going to throw some questions at us. They'd like to know just what we're doing here. They're right in not trusting us: We don't have the slightest intention of putting our fate in their hands; we didn't even ask for permission to enter. We just looked for a way of going directly to the playing fields. And we found it. It was that simple.

Sometimes it was simple to get away. Once two of us were crossing a bridge lugging a big box containing a mimeograph machine and a couple of guns. I don't recall exactly why, but at the far end there was a soldier, outfitted to the hilt, like he was going off to World War II. He taps the package with the tip of his rifle. "What's in there?" he inquires. "A mimeograph machine and a couple of guns," is my reply. Then the guy just chuckles and waves us on. "Go right ahead." The trick worked like a charm. In any case, if he'd decided to search it, at least we wouldn't have been caught lying.

At least they don't lie to us. They inform us that we have to submit to questioning by the Federal Police for having bypassed the security system.

Security agents come around and inquire where we're staying. "We don't have a place yet," we admit. "We were planning to find a hotel near the railroad station." "Come with me, I can take care of that," shoots back one low-ranking officer, and we aren't sure if that means he's taking us to jail. We follow, and he offers to put us up in one of the classrooms of the police academy. We stay there, surrounded by blackboards, benches, and uniforms.

The following morning he invites us to go for a walk in Tafí del Valle. We're a bit queasy about this, but we accept. As we meander along we come across a cow standing right on the path. The guy shoos her away, pulls out his gun, aims at her head, and fires. That's the end of the cow and of our serenity. He sneers at our look of revulsion.

Trying our best to look as innocent as babes in arms, we explain to one of the inquisitors: "We didn't bypass anything, sir. The gate was opened for us, and it was locked behind us after we entered. They let us in without uttering a single word."

Kiryat Shmonah

"Go ahead and ask."

"OK, here's the question. What's the meaning of *lehistakel?*"

You draw the caricature of a midget with a penis the size and shape of a club. A woman is staring at it, her eyes about to pop out of her head.

"The act of looking."

"Ten points, *havera, meah achuz,* my friend!"

Patricia and Nora make hundreds of cards to illustrate the main verbs in Hebrew. The guttural *R*s get entangled in their giggles, and for a while they're able to forget about life at Kiryat Shmonah, its bell-regulated monotony. Chat-time bell, lunch bell, et cetera—bell, bell, bell. Bells to muffle other sounds hovering over the landscape.

As I return from a walk the city lies in darkness, the streets deserted. Before I have a chance to figure out what's happening, someone drags me to the shelter where Nesia, the teacher, unfazedly continues her lesson on irregular verbs. The building shakes, shots echo, the earth groans. Nesia, meantime, erects the screen of her indifference right before us. It's contagious. When we reemerge, we watch as soldiers deactivate a *katyusha,* a rocket that's made the long, fast trip from Lebanon. They find it buried in our street—a black hole in the asphalt of our swift introductory course.

"We slipped in so swiftly that we can't recall all the details. A man in civilian clothes came up driving a truck that seemed to belong to the Army. He got out, opened the gate, and locked it behind us. If you call the police, we'll call the Canadian Embassy. Just to save time," Kerrie and I state in unison.

Florence

Calling an embassy doesn't always save time. Occasionally there are more direct ways to reach a country, ways that may lie unseen around corners, in secret crevices, or in gardens.

In that particular garden I was reading Onetti under the shade of a climbing vine, which offered some protection from the uncertainty evoked by *The Body Snatchers*. I wasn't at all sure whether I was in Florence or Santa María, whether I was waiting for Gabriel or had landed in some imaginary city. All I knew was that the book soothed other, more piercing doubts that plagued my dreams.

"Ti va di bere un cappuccino?"

Why not? For the first time in a week someone interrupts my steely resolve of denying reality with the help of the printed word. All at once I wake up to a warm morning amid rolling hills and vineyards, and I agree to have some coffee with this man, in all likelihood the owner of the mansion. The problem is that our chat ejects me from my parenthesis and into a world that requires explanations: where I come from, where I'm going. It's not easy to engage in conversation when one is intent on avoiding the edges of the present. How do I tell him that past and future are borders for which I have no visa?

Carlo persists: *"Cosa facevi prima di venire?"* I'm not even sure exactly how I crossed the border into this welcoming mansion. All I remember is that I followed the instructions of the friend for whom I'm waiting and sought shelter. "Before coming here" is a remote concept in an unknown language. He, on the other hand, is able to give a precise account of his life: a professor at the University of British Columbia, he comes to Florence every summer to visit his mother, and in August he returns to

Vancouver to teach literature. A rhythmical life, with cycles as predictable as the seasons. From his collection of certainties, he questions me once more. This time I opt for a sassy answer.

"I have no plans, but I'm open to suggestions. So make me an offer."

Most men delight in the role of guide, of teacher, of redeemer, particularly if they get to play it opposite a young woman who's fragile, disoriented, lost. As soon as Carlo sees that opportunity, he doesn't hesitate:

"Vieni a studiare in Canada," he ventures as if in a question-and-answer game show.

Why argue? Italians are capable of promising anything just to charm a tourist. Eager to put an end to this exchange, I give him an address where he can send me the application for admission to his prestigious institution.

"Maybe it can all be settled on an international level. The Canadian Embassy can deal directly with the ESMA. What do you think?"

Kerrie nods: finally an agreement.

I cannot come to an agreement with myself about which course of action to take. From Israel to Spain: meeting Andrés, who turns out not to be the man of my dreams. From Spain to Italy: meeting a man who lures me to study in Canada. From Italy to Brazil: 1980, meeting my parents to greet the New Year; not so happy, but at least the one starting isn't even-numbered. From Brazil to England: planned meeting with Patricia, my double. One pays dearly in every way for all these comings and goings, but my memory's accountant insistently records my expenses in the column of disappointments.

London

Airline schedules can be frustrating when passengers coming in from different countries have international appointments. My intercontinental meeting with Patricia swings between the fifteenth and the eighteenth of July 1981. Since you're coming from Jerusalem and I from São Paulo, we agree to meet halfway, in London. I arrive on the afternoon of the seventeenth. You had arrived earlier. I dial your number in the din of a train station.

"I'm sorry, Patricia's gone," says an English accent.

How am I to believe this disembodied, deceitful voice? How can I accept that shameless voice that has the nerve to distort the facts like that? I dial again.

"She left this morning. She thought you weren't coming. I've no idea where she went."

You're gone. Without leaving a message, a trace, or even a piece of scrap paper, like those we pushed into the Wailing Wall to share jokes with Jehovah. I look for you, unable to believe that you would disappear of your own free will. There's no point. From now on, your name too will be an absence. An absence surrounded by cats, sketches, paintbrushes, jars, rags. An absence with a green gaze, spellbound by the cactus growing out of the stone, by an abandoned dog, by the sound of a drop of water falling on the pond, by an aroma wafting through the street. An absence with magical hands creating characters in the air. You get erased, like those figures you drew on the walls of your bedroom, whitewashed by the landlord, leaving barely a trace. Perhaps a blurred profile peering through the paint, vainly determined to survive.

I'm determined to keep up my fear-induced, self-sufficient tone before the ESMA inquisitors, and I request a telephone. The long delay has made me late for a very important appointment. I need to cancel it.

Toronto

I have a very important appointment with a Canadian immigration officer. I'm determined to make myself understood in my rustic English, but I come to the conclusion that language is not the problem. As soon as our dialogue gets under way, I see that he's incapable of following the map of my exile. My routes leave officials thoroughly confounded, accustomed as they are to a certain coherence between nationality and territory.

SENIOR IMMIGRATION OFFICER: Are you Nora Strejilevich?

N.S.: Yes, sir.

S.I.O.: According to your application form, you're a citizen of Argentina by birth?

N.S.: Yes, sir.

S.I.O.: And prior to coming to Canada, you were a resident there also, is that correct? You were residing in Argentina?

N.S.: Just before coming? No.

S.I.O.: Where were you living?

N.S.: I was in Brazil, and then I came here. I was living in several countries. I left Argentina five years ago.

S.I.O.: Five years ago?

N.S.: Yes, sir.

S.I.O.: And you were living in Brazil, prior to coming to Canada?

N.S.: Prior, yes. And before that, I had been in other places, but prior to coming to Canada, I was there.

S.I.O.: How long were you in Brazil?

N.S.: Approximately eight months. Approximately.

S.I.O.: What was your status there?

N.S.: Just visitor-tourist.

S.I.O.: So you are not claiming refugee status from Brazil?

N.S.: No, sir.

S.I.O.: How many countries have you lived in prior to living in Brazil?

N.S.: Israel, Spain, England, and Italy.

S.I.O.: And you were there just temporarily?

N.S.: Yes.

S.I.O.: And you are not claiming refugee status from any of those countries you have mentioned?

N.S.: No.

S.I.O.: I want to read you the definition of a Convention Refugee, as it appears in the Immigration Act: Convention Refugee means a person who, by reason of a well-founded fear of persecution for reasons of race, religion, nationality, membership in a particular social group or political opinion . . . is outside the country of his or her former habitual residence and is unable or, by reason of such fear, unwilling to return to that country. Do you understand the definition as I have read it?

N.S.: Yes.

S.I.O.: Are you unwilling or unable to return to Brazil for fear of persecution because of your race?

N.S.: Brazil is not my country, just the country I'm coming from.

S.I.O.: I understood Brazil.

N.S.: I said Argentina.

S.I.O.: I don't think so.

N.S.: Yes.

S.I.O.: Yes, sir.

N.S.: Yes, sir.—Interview to request political asylum, Toronto, 1982

Yes, sir, I request asylum in order to stop living in a territory where seasons and moods don't coincide. But my mood plummets when proof of persecution is requested. Actually, there is a witness to my wounds: a doctor I saw right after I was released from the Athletic Club. I need her to provide the Canadian Embassy with a statement to that effect. She says she'll do it from abroad. She's about to leave for Europe, and she'll mail a letter from there. Time passes. No letter arrives, and I inquire once more. She says she talked it over with her husband and that she can't do it, even if strict confidentiality is guaranteed. She never sends it.

A Navy recruit is sent to escort me to the telephone. Followed by his olive green shadow, I enter a room where I can make a call. I dial the number of James Petras, an American sociologist with whom I had scheduled an interview that afternoon. As soon as he picks up the receiver, I explain the situation, always in English and speaking at breakneck speed. I ask him to remember my name in case I do not turn up later that day. I tell him I'm calling from the ESMA. He can scarcely believe his ears, but he takes note.

Sarita

I can scarcely believe the accent I hear on the telephone. A call in Spanish finds me in my English-speaking world. What's going on? They urge me to return to Buenos Aires before you have surgery, Mama, that very Friday. I walk my anguish by the ocean, to air it out in the evening mist. The seagulls know that I'll be on the first plane out. By definition, a refugee cannot go back to the country that she is fleeing, but definitions often do not fit life. Aboard the plane I leaf through your letters. Your handwriting chisels a volatile sculpture into my memory.

6 December 1983

Dearest daughter,

I've read that when he sculpted Moses' face, Michelangelo wanted to capture and give expression to the leader's conviction that his people should not destroy themselves, that they should accept and obey commandments carved onto the tablets, that they should survive. One must keep going and accept the circumstances even when one feels that part of one's existence is being left behind or lost.

It's like surgery: the defunct or diseased organ is removed, the skin is sewn up, a scar forms, and the absence of the organ is not noticeable from outside. In short, "everything" continues to work. Everything continues to work as it should.

The ESMA inquisitors do not call the police. Instead, they usher us into an office. In the hallway, a cluster of ancient typewriters. Inside, a wooden desk, paintings of ships and stormy seas, a couple of file cabinets, shelves. Three blue uniforms whose flawless, sparkling, polished smiles smother my soul.

I try to stay calm despite the clouds smothering my soul; I seek buttonholes in the sky onto which I can fasten my distress. They say that your condition is terminal, but never out loud, and the whispers are stifling me. There are words that hide inside others, like tiny pebbles. The word *cancer* is never mentioned over the phone.

The journals, which I assumed contained medical information, turn out to be military handbooks:

CANCER CELLS INVADE, colonize, destroy. The body's defenses are not strong enough to eradicate the malignancy. Even with radical surgery, the invasive tumor may continue to grow. Therapy kills the cancer cells through chemical warfare. It's not possible to spare healthy cells, but any damage done to the body seems justified if it succeeds in saving the life of the patient.

In a different way this has to do with war, with armies. Let's just say that the Army bombarded you with the word *desaparecido.*

"It will kill a lot of parents," you predicted.

And here you are, in a hospital bed.

It's already happened

The buttonholes finally unfasten under your hands' eternal gesture.

> *Your impossible hand gathers me*
> *from unbearable distances*
> *knitting itineraries*
> *that my words gently unknit.*

> *Your nocturnal hand in my morning*
> *combs my memories*
> *ringlets of rhymes*
> *curl sweetly around your fingers.*

> *Your hand, a snail, slowly traces*
> *the edges of my childhood*
> *while I watch my own palm caressing*
> *the profile of pain.*

A pain soothed by your words of old.

"You're no longer a child; you're growing wings. We'll be three beings linked by genuine love. A closed unit."

The three Navy officers act as a unit. Each one seems to recite a part of the speech, but it's really the institution doing the talking.

"We want to know why you came to the ESMA, why you entered through a side door. Imagine if we were to enter your house through the backyard. You might just take us for thieves."

I'm a thief of words, Mama. I copy yours, even though you didn't make good on your promise: "Don't worry about me: I'll survive in spite of my ghosts. Besides, nothing more can happen to us: IT ALREADY HAS."

That must be the reason nothing ever happens to them. The Joint Command entered our house through the main door, and no one thought anything of it. These men are speaking with the voice of experience. We, however, seem like petty thieves, amateurs unfamiliar with the basic rules of impunity: act in broad daylight, without worrying about covering your tracks.

You covered up all traces of the word *cancer*. For years you kept it tucked under your pillow and tried to survive without saying much. Around the time elections were called, you allowed it out of hiding but never actually spoke it aloud because that's taboo. The sanctioned word, *illness*, has grown to such proportions that it now leaves no room for me to talk to you: I'm prevented by questions that stick in my throat, faltering on the edge of your fevers and therapies. Questions stand guard by your side, counting each flutter of your eyelids, keeping track of your dreams: What do the eyes of death look like? Will she leave a pair behind before vanishing?

Questions yearn to uncover everything. They long to learn what you know, to turn themselves around and become answers, to stand up so you can stay on your feet, to lie down with you, embrace you. The hospital call button isn't working, so the nurse doesn't answer; a massive weight, the patient on the neighboring bed, invariably collapses on top of your slight silhouette each time she gets up; the doctors miss their rounds; Papa cannot locate the words "don't give up" in any of his drawers, which is normal in such cases.

Not knowing when or how, I draw close to your sensed eternity. I gaze at the bedside of your world as if I were spying on a temple that I didn't dare enter. I keep a sketch of your profile outlined against the pillow, holding all the answers. I take you home.

We are the owners of life and death

Home. That is, until they show up, the usual crowd. The ones who give the orders, who decide on your behalf in the name of Science, of Order, of Religion. Whichever.
"I'd rather let myself die. I won't go back to the hospital."

"I won't be interrogated," I repeat to myself, when I realize that's precisely what's in store for us. Faced with the initial question, Kerrie once more displays her customary bouquet of topics: human rights, the dead, the newspaper article about kids playing ball in a place like this. She's playing the journalist. And what about me, what do I play?

I play spectator, since I have no strength to challenge Papa. He opens the door and three smocks lift you, submissive, defeated, huddled in your chair / beaten, overpowered, they drag you / the ambulance screeching time / we arrive, the stretcher, those eyes, don't pierce me with those eyes / helpless / good-bye, good-bye / this arsenal of tears / your pupils dart about / they look at me without seeing / stay, come back, don't go just yet / your broken, undulating movements / your arms waving about, clutching at the void / terror lacerates me / I won't be the one to cover up your face / trapped in a net of reflections. I leave.

That was yesterday. Today
your hand no longer speaks to me
and I stroke the womb of your absence
that began just a quiver ago.

So I invent a double for your hand
tattooed in the space for consolation
a mirror to recover the shape of your gestures
on the threshold of oblivion.

Silence is health

Trapped on the threshold of memory, I gape in astonishment at a familiar scene: the customary *milico* addressing me from the other side of the desk, from the absolute other side. Will he end up saying that he's sorry, that it was all a mistake?

Now I can see what's happening, not just hear it. And what I hear takes unsuspected turns thanks to Kerrie, who, by virtue of quoting facts from international newspapers about concentration camps, sweeps away the symmetry of memories. The Navy officers cannot hide their surprise before the journalist's earnestness. Is it a mistake to hammer away at these topics? Is silence health? A smirk cloaks a certain (nervous?) smile on their faces each time the word *desaparecidos* is spoken. I'd swear they salivate, like Pavlov's dog, but I couldn't prove it.

Kerrie speaks now about the Mothers. Does she need to mention them here and now?

> DESPITE THE TIME ELAPSED, the Mothers continue clamoring for violence, airing their grievances, hurling insults, and trying to incite many peace-loving Argentines to enter the realm of violence.—Statement from President Menem, 4 May 1994

"Don't for a minute believe a word the Mothers say," Scheller, the Navy officer, warns me. "All of that happened twenty years ago, anyway, and it was a war with casualties on both sides."

> A WAR HAD BEGUN, an oblique, different kind of war, primitive in its ways but sophisticated in its cruelty, a war to which we gradually became accustomed because it wasn't easy to admit that the entire country was being forced into a monstrous intimacy with blood. Then the battle began. Surmounting all obstacles, the Armed Forces went on the offensive. This is a war between dialectic materialism and idealistic humanism. We're

fighting against nihilists, against agents of destruction disguised as social crusaders. Because all of our dead, each and every one, died for the triumph of life.—Emilio Massera, *La Nación*, 11 March 1976

Here no one dies when he wants to
or lives because he wants to

Hope has died for you, Papa. You scarcely manage to ramble your circular monologue around the blueprint of your past, trying to clear up the errors. The design of your youthful days has developed cracks, and now, with shaking hands, you're intent on correcting flawed lines. The balance is unfavorable: no more son, no more wife, a daughter who comes only to leave again. You don't go out much, you don't share your despair with others, you don't fight a public fight. You lack faith. No wonder you underlined in red that passage from Cortazar's *Rayuela*:

> I HAD NO FAITH that what I wanted would happen, and I knew that without faith nothing ever happens. I knew that without faith what should happen never does, and with faith it usually doesn't either.

"You can't put your faith in what newspapers say, either. There are lots of unfounded accusations out there in an effort to discredit the Armed Forces. Foreign correspondents ought to listen to both versions."

My version of you, Gerardo, is a solid and imposing body leaning over the balcony railing as if seeking more space. Spindly beard, cigarette in hand, a slight grin as if telling yourself a private joke.

What joke might that be? You never answer my questions. I count myself lucky if you linger by the foot of my bed whenever you're in need of an ear and some pampering. But what about me? Come on, tell me things. Nothing. Your eyes look at me, but you keep silent.

Scheller—his last name is German, he mentions twice—lets his eyes meander without undue haste over Kerrie's passport pages. He seasons each glance with a question.

My questions that morning, Papa, assumed it was a day like any other. Where you were going, when you would be back. You seemed composed, focused. You were going over to my uncle's. I was going to be busy into the afternoon.

That evening, the surprise of a sheet of notebook paper, written with trembling hand and slipped under the front door, greets me on arrival. I pick it up in the darkness and sit down to read it. The letters crush me.

30 March 1987

Señorita Nora:

Please come immediately to your Aunt Rosita's house, if at all possible before 7:00 A.M. tomorrow, 31 March.
    It's a VERY URGENT matter concerning YOUR FATHER.

"Child, your father . . . here in our building . . . from the third floor . . . the stairs that lead to the inner courtyard . . . we didn't realize . . . he asked the doorman to let him in . . . they came to get us . . . I don't know what to say to you . . . you have to be questioned by the police . . . I've already told them a few things . . . You have to go."

We have all the time in the world

At the Navy School of Mechanics I have to submit to questioning in front of a desk, in front of those who always have the right to ask.

"And you," he grunts and adjusts his angle of vision, "do you live here?"

"No."

"No? What year did you leave?"

"1985."

My head is about to explode from all the blank-faced lying. Why would I have left after the dictatorship was over?

Right when my head was about to explode from thinking so hard, it suddenly occurred to me exactly what we, the Mothers, were seeking. We wanted to recover lives, wrest them from their control, while what they wanted was fog, silence, and above all oblivion. I remember a film about the Holocaust, Shoah, in which the Nazis would say, "Schneller, schneller, faster, faster." They were supposed to carry out their massacres swiftly, leaving no traces. The ones here also want to leave no trace. Their goal, when they "disappear" a person, is to leave nothing behind, to rub out even the name. I tried to fathom what a captive person might think, cooped up and isolated like that, in the gloom of night, knowing that very likely no one would ever see him or her again. It must be something like, "No one will ever know where I was, where they killed me. They erased me from the world; they erased me completely."

I thought to myself, "At some point this man has to get something to eat, has to go home, has to have a life." They knew what I was thinking, because they'd say, "I have to go sometime, but someone else will come to take my place. We've all the time in the world; no one knows where you are."

You're no longer here, Papa. You jumped into the void, and your pocket watch split in two.

The concept of someone

Splitting me in two with his gaze, the Navy officer resumes his questioning:

"What's your address in Buenos Aires?"

"I don't have one; I'm just passing through."

"Are you staying with someone?"

"Are you looking for someone?" I hear at the cemetery.

This city is no less a city just because it's eternal. With trees, streets, neighborhoods. And guards. One of these tireless sentinels approaches. He doesn't recognize my face but seems to sniff out the fact that I'm not from around here. I let some time elapse between his question and my answer. I'm afraid of how it will come out. I try to tune my vocal chords to avoid screaming, and in the meantime I hear his voice once more. A cone-shaped echo tickles me with its tip. Am I looking for someone? Laughter almost bursts out of me, but I manage to hold it inside, clinging to the walls of my guts. Let him wonder. I'm not about to regale this respectable gentleman with some exquisite philosophical tidbits about the concept of someone.

"Are you staying with someone?" Scheller repeats.

"No, I'm by myself."

"Don't you have a family?"

I'm not about to explain that I misplaced the map to your grave, or that I never kept it because the image of the Virgin on the cover was way too absurd. What a pity. It's just not the same to remember the scene without that feminine profile, adorned with a sparkling halo set against a rainbow. Flawless: a Virgin with vacant eyes observing your departure. Why not?

"Religion?" I was asked when filling out the form for making arrangements.

"Atheist," I answered. "I don't want anything: no hearse, no flowers, no cards. A-the-ist," I repeated, to make it perfectly clear.

"But the insurance company is picking up the tab, señora. Not a penny comes out of your pocket."

"Señorita. And I don't want anything." I was afraid you'd tease me if I gave in to the temptation of rites. You might even make faces during the glumness of your own funeral. It was way too risky to let myself be carried along by the habit of turning a deaf ear to your sermons.

The person questioning me turns a deaf ear to my memories:

"Husband? Children? Father? Mother?"

I'll skip our family's saga, lest he should get sentimental.

People tend to get sentimental at funerals. When Mama died, an aunt scolded us for forsaking her ashes in the public space. We simply scattered them, turned them loose out in the open, so they could fly about freely.

He's not going to let us out of the ESMA unless I say something that satisfies him. I could always make up a story, no big deal. He won't be sending it to the newspapers, anyway.

I do not send the obituary to the newspapers, because showing up among the deceased would have seemed to you in poor taste, a pathetic way of becoming known at the wrong time.

No ceremonies to help close the wounds. Let mine remain wide open. Death and its turns. I build no monuments for you, but I carry you in my body, in my cells, in my feet. I take you for the walks that you so direly need. Along the way I tell you the conclusion of your own story.

"It's a long story," I confess to the Navy officer. "The short of it is that I'm all alone."

A solitary blue van parks in the designated space, and two men pull you out carefully. As the casket emerges, I spot a metal cross that cuts the wood into four segments. I tell myself that I'm imagining things, no doubt as a way to cope. I have nothing against crosses, you know that. But this is not the time to take up the semantic weight of the Jew on the cross. Oh, well. It's also not the time for questions. They unload you, put you in place, perform their role. Every play has an end, and then the curtain falls. Before lowering the casket into the ground, they hand me the card of the Virgin with a little map to locate your piece of underground heaven.

A keepsake! Like the ones you used to sell at market fairs when you were a kid! The bizarre symmetries of fate close the circle, and I cannot suppress a final smile.

They smile. I wonder if rehearsing that antiseptic smile is part of basic training, but then again I doubt that such instructions appear in any of their manuals.

Your atheism does not appear in their manuals. Those who are neither one thing nor the other are labeled Christian, or more specifically, Roman Catholic. I wonder which cubbyhole they fit you into. You made it to paradise by default, without going to confession or taking Holy Communion—unlike Videla, who does it regularly in order to guarantee his place in eternity. You were rewarded for not fearing the ever-after and now, having disappeared from our modest earthly spaces, you can relish your ethereal resting ground.

The office, as well as the Navy's uniform grammatical structures, closes in on me:

"Identification?"
"I don't think I have it with me."
"Could you get it?"

CAUTION

"I'm looking for my father. We buried him in 1987."
"The ones from '87 have been transferred."

We were transferred from the block that we'd occupied and moved to one with individual cells. There they divided us into two categories: those who had a sign on their door reading "CAUTION" and those who had a sign reading "SEMI-CAUTION." I recall that the signs were scrawled in chalk. If the sign read "CAUTION," the person was all alone in the cell because he or she was considered dangerous; if it read "SEMI-CAUTION," then there were two people in the cell. Later on, we were transferred from there too, and along the way a few more disappeared.

Here, as in any other city, those who cannot pay have to go. Wealthy sections have fabulous structures, adorned with curlicues and famous quotes. Poor suburbs, like this one, suffer the scourge of artificial flowers huddling over spindly wooden crosses. And dirt. Lots of dirt. They have disappeared you from the poorest neighborhood of the cemetery, the sticks almost. Transferred. To where?

"Where's my ID disappeared to?" I mutter like a fool before the Navy officer's stony face. I continue rummaging through my purse wearing an expression of utter bewilderment.
"Things sometimes disappear just like ghosts, don't they?" Scheller chimes in now, almost amused.

Things must be stripped of their ghostly air. I go back to the shores of my early wanderings, to the uninhabited apartment, in order to strip objects of their shadows; return them to the circle of hands and voices; restore to them a function, a practical purpose. Clothes hanging in closets, tablecloths embroidered by great-great-grandmothers, crystal wedding goblets, gargantuan trunks, dresses that exude ocean tides and exotic scents, baskets filled with menorahs, even a silver-bound Bible. All should be released to the adventure of life. I come to free you from these limits, the past and its sorrows. Am I right in letting you go? Have you perhaps grown accustomed to the stale air of these rooms of yours? I am sorry, I have no place to store you. What pocket could hold the silver, which bag could keep the books, where to put the little bronze statue of the newspaper boy? How to pack maps, coats, postcards, flatware, china teacups, dishes, knickknacks, sewing chests, musical scores, shelves? Since you were spared the glorious fate of being carried off as war booty, I ought to pile you onto a magic carpet and have you follow me around the planet—a caravan of curios hurtling through the cosmos, adrift. Just as I, adrift like you, hurtle through the immensity of space. But since I have to pay fares, I shall exchange you for base metals. You must understand, my dear friends. No, you simply cannot stay, I do regret it. It wouldn't be healthy. I have to leave you behind. In the twentieth century, with its calendar of exiles and meta-exiles, it's just not possible to cling to shapes, colors, sounds. "We keep the clothes in the closet, but we have not unpacked the suitcases of the soul." Not yet, Gelman.

I must go. They must go without ever having confided their secrets to me, those murmured under fedoras or black tulle. Europe is sold off cheaply in America, to the highest bidder. In the Argentina of the nineties even memories are privatized. Generations of Russians and Poles carried this arsenal of marvels, these splendid parcels, to the zenith of their destiny: sold at fabulous discounts—two pesos, cash and carry—in some South American market fair.

Tables have been generously spread throughout various rooms. Objects gather on them, classified according to function, price, or chance. Piles, pairs, single objects, each with its tag, always a modest price. Unique items for a song, an antique dealer's dream.

"Come on in, take it all away, just leave me your change!" The change of life, of country, of skin. I exchange history for consumption, one more history consuming itself.

"Come on in, don't pass up the curios."

Must have been into something

The curious thing is that the officer shows no sign of being annoyed by my lies: "OK, it doesn't matter; just tell me the number of your ID."

What number could I possibly dial to reach you, Gerardo? And what should I say when someone answers? I don't want to sound like those old ladies reciting the wonders of their children. How do I tell everyone that you're the most lovable, the most charming, the most intelligent, the grumpiest, the most alive, the very best friend I ever had?

Ladies and gentlemen, the one I'm looking for likes to strum the guitar, has a weakness for coffee, plays soccer and other sports, has been known to watch TV, and cooks much better than Mama ever did.

He's fond of camping and staying up all night, has friends in many different languages, travels the length of the continent, and writes poems at dawn.

He's about to finish his thesis about the permanence of matter, but he personally had no resistance to the metal scissors I threw at him when I was four years old. He's thinking of getting married.

He's an activist, calls himself an atheist but says an Our Father of his own making: let everyone have food, let everyone get an education, let everyone have choices. He must have been into something.

The one I'm looking for has eyes that speak, untamed hair, imposing height, a wavy voice, and childlike gestures.

The one I'm looking for has never grown old; his brow is not wilted, nor are his temples graying.

He delights in playing hide-and-seek, cowboys and Indians, King of the Mountain, and chess.

He teaches me to recite *My shoes are tight / my socks are not / and the guy up the street / is making me veeeeery hot.*

He's great at math but is incapable of drawing a cow. As a kid he locked himself in the bathroom, as an adolescent in his bedroom, and when he was grown they locked him in a camp.

He lives on in a black-and-white photo ID; in a color slide, rowing with T-shirt knotted, belly showing; in a notebook filled with mathematical formulas; in a pair of shoes; and in several concert programs autographed by the musicians.

Do you know where your child is right now?—TV ad during the dictatorship

We used to go to concerts, parties, clubs, cookouts. Gerardo would sing, make people laugh; he was always so much fun. So many times we camped, pulled pranks—practical jokes, that sort of thing. Sometimes he'd show off, but only a little. As a teenager he was kind of insecure, for which he compensated by acting cocky. Perhaps what happened a few years later was similar: he thought he was short on commitment, that he had to try harder and deepen his political involvement, to what extent I don't know.

I recall moments: Gerardo could strum a few songs really well on the guitar, bass and all. A group of girls who were about thirteen back then, and must be ninety by now, looked up to him as if he was some kind of movie star.

I remember a party at which he changed shirts about seven times. It was really hot, and every once in a while he appeared wearing a different outfit. "What's this, a fashion show?" I asked. It seems he was courting a girl and wanted to impress her with his shirt collection: striped ones, red ones, plaid ones . . . I was baffled and kept repeating, "What is this?"

Disappeared, but not entirely

"What is this?" Not a course schedule, no! It's a pamphlet! Kerrie and I are officiously handed twin information pamphlets about the school. She gets the one in full color, I receive the black-and-white version.

Man is free only when he has choices
Science, technology, future
You'll find it all at the
NAVY SCHOOL OF MECHANICS

At the high school where I was teaching we were required to take the students on field trips to towns created by the milicos. *We'd arrive there at whatever hour and knock. The residents were obliged to let us in and show us around. And then we would listen to their canned speech about how grateful they were to the armed forces of Argentina for having given them all that. They were jail-like towns, similar to those "strategic hamlets" in Vietnam, where the population was supposed to continually pay homage to the military for providing such a glorious fate. This farce was referred to as the eradication of rebellious segments of the population.*

When the population has to vote, each person must first consult the electoral lists. It's easy enough: you find the initial of your last name and use your index finger to go down endless sheets affixed to the wall of some government building. As a rule, you come to it and then verify exactly where you must go to exercise

your civic duty. I go to an old school building located at the inter-
section of Pueyrredón and Lavalle Streets and proceed according
to instructions.

Suddenly my finger feels drunk, sees double, triple images,
not one last name but four. I read them: Yes, they're here! Gerardo, Abel, Hugo . . . And why not? The mere fact that you disappeared doesn't mean that you ceased to be responsible for per-
forming your civic duty. You may have disappeared, but not
entirely! In order for you to lose the right to vote, it would have to
be proven that you're no longer around.

If they disappear, there must be a reason

In order to strut their didactic zeal, the officers explain that the
ship gracing the pamphlet is a frigate. As they speak, they lead us
to the entrance, and I step out onto the path without looking
back.

Why not go backwards, as in fairy tales?
Why don't you come back, brother?
Say something.

"Just let us know when you wish to come again, and we'll be
at your service, as usual," the officers reiterate obligingly.

Always the noises of the night. It seems my fate to hear them,
number them, struggle to distinguish among them that shrill,
boastful life force clamoring to make itself visible, like a beacon
in the foggy darkness of turbulent seas.
What sea were you referring to, Gerardo?

Our freshwater sea, that Río de la Plata into which you
plunged like a pendulum? Prisoners were taken on death flights
and thrown out over the open sea. Did your body approach the
shore like a beacon in the darkness? Were the waters turbulent?

Hermeneutics as a strident route toward despair.

Interpretation as a counterpoint to silence.

I came back, Gerardo, to tie up the loose ends of our story into a knot that might undo the uncertainty. To recover a version of the facts that could be pieced together and understood and believed. To free myself from the compulsion of inventing possible endings, endless possibilities. To turn you into a book whose ending I alone decree, whose ending is open and subject to change. Wishful thinking. What I found had nothing to do with literature: someone said you'd been shot, someone had seen you at the ESMA. ESMA—they shot Gerardo, they determined the end.

In the end, they see us to the door. But the exit is still blocked by their three immovable bodies.

WHY SHOULD THE BODIES DISAPPEAR?
Why should the bodies be destroyed? Was it on the same basis as an individual criminal trying to wipe out all traces of his act? We don't think this is sufficient explanation. There was something more . . . first it was the people . . . then the concealment and destruction of documentation . . . and finally the nameless bodies, without identity, driving people distraught at the impossibility of knowing the specific fate of their loved one. It was a bottomless pit of horror. Wiping out the identity of the corpses magnified the shadow hanging over the thousands of disappeared of whom all trace was lost after their arrest or kidnapping.—*Nunca Más*

No trace of their authoritarian ways of a few minutes ago. Such polite hosts! All that's missing is for them to ask for our addresses in Canada in order to send us a postcard. If they insist, I'll be sure to mail them one showing a blindfolded face, lest they forget about their kidnapped-murdered victims.

There are no limits—Motto of the ESMA task forces

In 1994 the former detained-disappeared were accorded legal existence and thus became eligible for reparations. I go back to the old building on Moreno Street, the Office of Human Rights, to have a firsthand look at the scene. From the third floor, I'm sent down to the first, and from the first back up to the third. There they explain that a person who claims to have been one of the *desaparecidos* must figure in some official document.

> *"If it's necessary to prove that I was one of the disappeared, I could go to the death camp and ask for an affidavit stating that I was kept there between 1976 and 1977," a former* desaparecido *told me when he came to request his share of reparation. He was an old man without a clue who spent a year locked up for no reason at all.*
> *"Please, sir, don't even think about doing that!" I implored him.*

The reason for requiring documentation is absolutely logical: you cannot be classified with any precision if there are no records of your being booked or released. In the end I'm still unclear whether the *desaparecidos* are or ever were, but one thing is certain: we will have to prove it.

> *I couldn't tell you whether I was detained, jailed, or disappeared. I don't show up anywhere; there's absolutely no record at all. Therefore I'm prevented from taking any sort of legal action.*

I'm allowed to start legal proceedings to request reparations. The government finally put an end to the not so methodical doubt of our existence and decreed that we are and we were. It seems they'll pay us for being who we are or were. The families of people who were what we were, but are not what we are, will also receive a sum of cash or bonds as compensation for the so-called forced disappearance (of their children, husbands, fathers, brothers, or other blood relatives). Putting it into the vernacular, you might say that we will be paid for having been illegally imprisoned and tortured and/or for having been murdered. But those terms are legally inoperative, literarily inept, and socially unacceptable.

What might count as a socially acceptable escape route from the ESMA? I signal for a taxi. So that it won't just drive by us, I wave as if taking my leave from the whole world.

"You'll see that the whole world will be on our side. It's just a matter of time. The main thing is letting the truth about the Navy School of Mechanics be known," Scheller keeps parroting, even as we slam the taxi door in his face.

The Ministry of Justice and Human Rights slams its door in my face, but with impeccable manners. I have decided to demand from the government the reparation it has finally offered to us, the former detained-disappeared. I spend half an hour in yet another hidden office, where I'm asked to have a seat and write down the basic information regarding my kidnapping: date, place, period of detention. I'm even offered a glass of water, a piece of paper, and a pen. This is 2001; the country has finally changed some of its old patterns, I tell myself while summarizing the essential data in a paragraph. At the end of my application I ask for reparations from the moment of my confinement to the present, since my whole life has been shattered by these "events." They inform me that I will get an official reply soon.

Ministry of Justice and Human Rights

Buenos Aires, 8 March 2001

In my capacity as Technical Coordinator of the Executive Unit of Law Number 24.043 of the Subsecretariat of Human Rights, I am pleased to respond to your letter requesting an extension of the reparations provided by said law, for the mistreatment which you suffered during your illegal detention.

With respect to this matter . . . I hereby request that you inform us whether your inquiry is in reference to a payment of benefits for "serious wounds." . . . Serious wounds are characterized by irreparable damage through the absolute loss of an organ's functional capacity, not merely through a reduction or weakening of its performance.

The accepted term ILLNESS refers to the deterioration of health, of greater or lesser severity; though incurable, such sickness must occur in a form that can be diagnosed by a medical professional. The concept of illness includes physical as well as psychological pathology. . . .

Assuming your claim fits the above description, you should attach a certified copy of your clinical records from the detention center, any legal judgments that attest to your damages, or a clinical or medical history with the date corresponding to the period of time your claim covers, sent out from an official institution of health.

Too bad the Athletic Club didn't survive. If I'd been taken to the ESMA, I would have used my visit to ask for my medical report. But you never know. The fact that my brother may have been at the ESMA didn't make his case any easier. The claim I made for reparations after his disappearance seemed to lie in a hazy limbo for years. The usual pace, I thought, and I let it be. Meanwhile, many cases were being processed. Why not mine?

Finally the voice of the law spoke out with clarity: Gerardo Strejilevich committed fraud, and thus reparations to his family are not to be given. My brother's IDs, stolen by his murderers, are now being used for their petty crimes! Torturers stealing with pilfered identities! Business as usual, I concluded with the usual nausea. But before I had time to do something about it, another version came to the fore.

Since the early eighties the University of Buenos Aires had been following the path of a certain student who had neglected to return a physics book to the library. The student was Gerardo Strejilevich. My parents hastily informed the institution that their son had been kidnapped and had remained disappeared since 1977. Unfortunately, since the student himself had not returned, the book could not be returned either. But universities will not allow these crimes to remain unpunished. They kept searching for my brother to the very end, and the case was eventually turned over to the police. When I applied for reparations, I learned that certain crimes in my country are taken damned seriously.

My lawyer, after the usual struggle with this unbearable heaviness of being, succeeded in cleansing my brother's posthumous record.

12 November 2000

Dear Nora,

I spent the entire afternoon in different human rights offices before I finally found the documents. The problem is the following: Gerardo was under surveillance because of a police report indicating that he was accused of fraud and was to stand trial before Penal Judge Number 31. It's dated 16 December 1980, and this is a "problem" because, as you well know, he disappeared on 15 July 1977.

III

My name a climbing vine
got tangled
among syllables of death
DE   SA   PA   RE   CI   DO
gone
name never more
my name.

Devoid of subject
how do I conjugate myself?
how do I roam
the alphabet of my tears?
I was eyes probing yesterdays
I was hands clutching shreds
I was feet slipping
on electric lines.

How do I pronounce myself?
I was flesh among speeches
without exit   without traces
of where   or why
or when   or until when.

You will never be able to say it!
Never say yourself, I thought.
But you will write,
Yes, I will write
thousands of gs   of rs   of os
vicarious doodles
children of my mouth
whirlpools of desire
that once were names.

I will write
black whips to subdue
certain untamed capital letters
smothering my blood.
I will resist   you will resist
with first name   with last name
the shameless language
of oblivion.

Final chapter?

Don't forget to forget the forgetting.
—*Juan Gelman,* Unthinkable Tenderness

A woman who'd been reading my testimony, Circle of Love over
Death, *called up to say that she'd like to get together so she could
give me a hug. She seemed very moved, and added, "Let's do it before I finish your book, otherwise I might not have the nerve." We
met one morning, and she wanted to talk about the book. I wanted
to talk about the hug. "You wanted to hug me because you were
touched," I said. "You felt so stirred that you urgently needed to
embrace the person telling you all those things. I want you to know
that this is the hug that we were denied. Over and above the pain,
the torture, the mourning, all the evil that they wrought, they didn't
let us have even that."*

*I know a girl who was in the same death camp as her brother,
at the very same time. She survived, her brother did not. As long as
she lives she's going to ask herself, "Why didn't they grant us one
final embrace?" I hope that question remains alive for generations
to come.*

I cannot cling to the past; I have to let it pour out, in an ava-
lanche of scenes and voices. I'd like to let it escape so I can air
out that corner where I have so ill-fittingly lodged it. I want it to
have a more bearable existence. Therefore, while in Canada, I
decide to see a psychologist.

I spend a long time in the waiting room looking through ads
for holistic therapy and rehearsing speeches before I'm ushered
into the office of a guy who is the living image of a sixties intellec-

tual: round, wire-rimmed glasses, curly hair, forty-something. The choice could not have been more fortuitous for the occasion, I think, as I smile at him for lack of words.

He asks the standard question: "What brings you here?" I answer with a summary description of my case, in starts and stops, fumbling about, with some gaps, some chronological leaps of Olympic proportions, emotional ups and downs, ambivalence and oversights. Without going into excessive detail, I sketch an outline so we can proceed. I speak looking inward and am unaware of his reaction until, at the close of a lengthy monologue, my eyes alight on his.

"Are you crying?" I ask, as if to convince myself.

Yes, the doctor is crying. He has to take off his glasses and dry his tears, which shamelessly smear his face.

"It's not that bad, doctor, don't worry," I manage to mumble as I move closer to him and attempt to stem the pitiful flow of saline liquid.

Thanks to my first-aid, he composes himself. He gives me an appointment for another day, but not waiting for his diagnosis, I declare myself cured.

High up in the sky / immortal flag / a warrior eagle / full of pride / soars in triumphant flight / a wing of blue / the color of the sky / a wing of blue / the color of the sea. . . .

Somewhere between amused and perplexed, I find myself intoning patriotic songs learned in school. It's one way to ease distress. Now it's me up there, flapping up in the sky, flying south. Another trick is to chew on my obsessions, as if telling myself secrets, in order never to betray them.

I would wish to be like secrets / never to betray.
—Rainer Maria Rilke

Betrayal is something akin to opening the window of a prison cell: everyone wants to do it, but it's the rare person who actually succeeds. Those were Céline's words, and he should have known what he was talking about since he did it. Betrayal is easy. The challenge lies in finding the opportunity.

I gave you the opportunity, Roberto, the eccentric publisher of philosophy journals with whom I watered my twenties so we could grow chairs and shelves and dreams and laughter. Betrayal is easy. It's enough to draw those tacky curtains sold at a time when the world was still rose-colored for us. In the semidarkness of maturity all cats are gray. Youthful ideals are much too shiny: they seem laminated, see-through now. Truth is murky, and the sooner you come to accept it, the sooner you can get on with business.

Money makes the world go 'round, the world go 'round . . .

Pity that we romantics, choked on the dimensions of our feelings and the volume of our emotions, should lose the measure of time. One must make haste. The only remedy for sadness is a fast read: a bird's-eye view, swifter than deception itself. It's not so hard; deception works at a leisurely pace, and watered only infrequently, it takes years to bloom. But it finally bears fruit, huge heavy fruit that falls from its own weight. Mine falls in the form of words that sound like tears against walls of silence.

You're Samsa

The walls of the apartment on Corrientes Street are made of silence, of bricks defiantly fighting off the dampness that corrodes them. Four missing people make for seven empty rooms in which dust and oblivion exist side by side. Wearied by so much neglect, absences shroud themselves with the cobwebs that adorn mounds of objects. When they bolt and run down the endless corridor, I catch them in my room in Vancouver and twirl them about in the air. Moths that perish, crashing into the lightbulb of my insomnia, troubled for not having given you a chance.

But I did give you, Roberto, enough occasions to disappoint me. The fault lay with our glorious youth, or rather, with believing in it. Those twenties of ours, brimming with duets of laughter, liberally seasoned with extravagant meals on apple crates. Warm cushions embroidered with complicity. Such images cloud my vision, but as our figures dissolve, I'm able to see that the metamorphosis was already in progress. You are Gregor Samsa, Kafka's beetle, and you're not exactly in an early stage of metamorphosis.

12 January 1979

Dearest daughter,

Since you asked for news of Roberto, I'll tell you a story. This morning he came by to take me to lunch. While we were eating, I talked about how man is able to change matter with the aid of a mathematical formula, that is, by means of an idea derived from it.

He mentioned an idea of his for manufacturing envelopes in which letters would arrive sooner, and without any waste of paper. He was so absorbed in the topic that he lost track of time and had to rush off. He flew out, as usual, on the wings of his briefcase. He didn't wait for the bill.

Papa was mistaken, Roberto. You had it in you to wait. You waited for Shush and Sarita to die. Then you offered to take care of things, that is, to oversee the sale of the apartment. Our home was sold, and you flew out as usual, on the wings of your briefcase. Flights on stuffed briefcases stay low; such piles of bills don't let you soar.

Open sesame

High up in the sky . . . I've got to stop singing: the plane that's bringing me back to my own story stops in transit. It lands in Santiago, Chile: "52°F, clear skies." I'm walking past a window that reads "Passport Control" when a voice, far less friendly than the accent, stops me in my tracks:

"What are you doing in Chilean territory?"

The official throws the book at me, threatening me with regulations and the technical meaning of the word *transit,* which by definition excludes the act of going through passport control and entering a country.

How do I explain that I'm lost in memories of walls and metamorphoses? My reflexes save me: I whip my professional badge out of my purse, like an actor in one of those Hollywood series wields a weapon, swiftly and not without a touch of irony.

Dr. Nora Strejilevich, Latin American Literature
University of British Columbia, Canada

The magic wand, the certificate of success, printed, of course, in an English designed to make bureaucratic eyes glitter. Open sesame. Unaware that my title of doctor is not the kind that cures, he reacts with a welcoming smile. Everything will be smoothed over without any glitches. "Follow me, doctor, no problem."

Fortunately, I'm no longer a lump that can be shredded with sharp and cutting statutes.

I let myself dissolve into the sticky magma of passengers who drift by, into the imprecise horizon of the landless. I go back to my assigned seat, in the assigned airplane, from the assigned country, and fill out the assigned customs form. But on takeoff I discover a disconcerting piece of information: today is not the seventeenth, my lucky number, not even the twenty-fifth, to which my superstitious logic has assigned second place. I'm arriving on an unlucky date! Landing on the twenty-fourth is dreadful, an offense to my much tattered existential calendar. Even numbers ruin my complicity with dates, leaving me and the country out in the cold. So it comes as no surprise, after landing on solid ground, that telephones are out of order, that taxi drivers buzz around like flies, and that a pair of winter boots protect my feet from 86°F and 80 percent humidity. Blame it on the twenty-fourth.

On the phone a voice rattles off the refrain of the national folklore: "Imagine, I couldn't even file a complaint because they were all out of forms at the police station!" My legs go soft in a wordless collapse. Just give me but one firm spot on which to stand, and I won't rock the boat! A newspaper and magazine stall comes into view. To camouflage my thorough state of bewilderment, I stare intently at the merchandise. Let's see if I can still read Spanish.

TODAY is the seventeenth anniversary of the military coup of 1976.

Either I can no longer read and my imagination is playing tricks on me or I do know how to read and, for the first time in my disconcerting life, the *milicos* are giving me an unintended satisfaction.

HUMAN RIGHTS organizations are calling for an open-mike radio session to be held at the corner of Diagonal and 9 de Julio from 8:00 A.M. to 8:00 P.M.

The most auspicious of seventeenths! I savor the news:

"THE COUP was an unavoidable act that had the support of practically all Argentine citizens, and little opposition except from subversive elements of society," stated the second president of the regime that began in 1976, Roberto Viola. Despite being found guilty of grave human rights violations and sentenced to 16 years in prison, cut short by the amnesty granted him and other military chiefs from that regime by President Menem, Viola affirmed that during the years known as "The Process" there was no governmental terrorism: the expression "institutionalized terrorism" simply does not fly.—*Clarín*, 24 March 1993

I'm shocked, not so much by the stern tone in which the uniformed voices speak as by the fact that they continue asserting themselves so smugly. Such an overbearing mode should have gone out of style. Of course, you never know with fashion. The times when each season featured just one or two distinctive colors are over; now anything goes, even khaki. Since I've just landed, I'm taken aback by this permissive style; let's hope I don't catch it and get used to it. Even though it would require years of training, it's an achievement that demands continual practice in order to be good at it. Among the people who gather around me at the newsstand I perceive nothing of the old rage, of that former simmer that words more subtle than these could easily have turned up to a boil twenty years before. They don't even bat an eye. But wait! A matron in her fifties is reaching absentmindedly for a copy of *Clarín*. The bill that she hands the clerk will give her access to the mischief of our teachers of semantics and to the exchange rate of the dollar, though that is not precisely a hot topic these days since lately the peso and the dollar float together like Siamese twins. I concentrate my hopes on the woman, expecting her blood to boil when she notices the headlines and reads over the article. Damn, was I wrong. The woman merely asks for change.

IN ORDER TO BELONG to the Amnesiacs' Club, no special talent is necessary, not even any great lapse of memory, be it spontaneous or caused by blows, by the aging of the arteries, or by poor blood flow to the brain, because our point of departure is the fact that from the moment of birth we're all amnesiacs, particularly those who think they do remember.—*Peri Rossi, "El club de los amnésicos"*

Always Coca-Cola

We're not all amnesiacs. We, the so-called survivors, are going back today to the grounds of the Athletic Club. Long ago I thought I glimpsed the gate through a keyhole. There are no keyholes now, just this barrenness criss-crossed by roads. In the now empty lot the wind stirs up clouds of dust around a café with red-and-white market umbrellas that read "Always Coca-Cola." That makes sense: if there's always Coca-Cola, there will often be Athletic Clubs. Coca-Cola forever, an essential ingredient for Athletic Clubs. That sign is worth a whole volume of political economy, my feet are saying as they tread over clumps of impotence. An impotence that launches a string of rhetorical questions: Is it still the same space? If there are no stairs, no peepholes, no guards, if the walls are gone, if cells and corridors lie buried under the merciless whir of expressways, then is it still the same space?

"It used to be a club, and now it's become a road. Pretty symbolic, right? They demolished it and paved a road in its stead." A road paved over our bodies suspended in a space that's no longer ours.

But there's always a "but" after the full stop: as the hours go by, the here-and-now starts to belong to us. Subtle, telltale signs emerge, keys to a landscape that at first looks banal. A sign reads, "This is the site of the Athletic Club." People are writing on the neighborhood walls, "Murderers." They play music.

Compañeros / *We've come here today* / *to tell stories* / *because they never could* / *vanquish our memories.* / *It was twenty years ago* / *on a very dark night,* / *one 24th of March* / *that the dictator-ship began.*

Amnesia-erasing hands labor, and the bricks begin to speak. The walls start to reflect white kerchiefs, spray-painted signs begin to demand justice. Even though it looks nothing like my yesterday, the place starts to make some sense.

I walk up and down the path taking pictures. I want to settle the score with this elusive landscape devoid of any points of reference by capturing angles, curves, and planes that might evoke a memory. I won't resign myself to not penetrating the geometry of my past; I'm intent on making a record of it, but I lose. What I mean is, I lose the camera. Literally and irreparably, out of carelessness or by dint of sheer clairvoyance, I lose the camera, and with it photos, frames, focus. I'm left in a fog of uncertainty that the sound of my footsteps cannot overcome. Objects are sometimes wiser than people. My camera has left me with nothing but my eyes.

What do you see?

I see, I see. What do you see? I see splashes of emerald green above the gray cement. The green climbs up a column, and I see green leaves with cloud-colored shadows. The columns hold up the highway, the one that was laid out in 1978 to airbrush the prison camp and the cattle prods. But names cannot be paved over, I tell myself, nor can souls. Names and souls have shapes that I can make out, the papier-mâché figures on the columns. I see the shape of time in exhausted wrinkles etched onto faces with India ink. The shape of pain on blindfolds over disappeared eyes. The shape of anger in tempera-painted mouths that refuse to speak. The shape of power in arms and fists upraised in stylized gestures. The shape of life in eyes open to the beyond. A bouquet of sculpted foreheads and profiles sprouts new green growth that reaches up to the base of the highway above and quivers in the breeze. They are the untamed spaces of history.

It's the birthday of our second skin, almost two decades old, and we celebrate it here, at the ruins of the Athletic Club. The laws of memory and of life demand our presence. That's why it seems appropriate to fill this space with wine, hugs, photographs, music, and poetry. Splashes of green blot out all possible blackness, and the apathy of the dust, while the wind plays in our hands. Hands that build a bonfire, fed by printed faces, profiles, and names of torturers consumed behind lengths of taut rope. Strange rituals beckon to us. A witch hunt? No. This is a party that breaks into cheerful songs and gathers around a barbecue while a paper nightmare goes up in flames.

I once ran into Julián the Turk on the street. He was strolling downtown with a kid on his shoulders. Perhaps for that reason I didn't feel like punching him. "Hi Tito," he called out to me. He dug one hand into his pocket, pulled out a pack of subway tokens, and said, "I'm really broke, man. Look here, I'm selling tokens to put some food on the table." I replied, "Do you remember what I told you once in the hellhole? You're like a condom, thoroughly disposable." He went on: "With all you know, you must've found yourself a pretty good job somewhere." I told him no, but that I was managing fine without his help. "I can refer you to some important people. You can say I sent you," he persisted. Then I asked him whether I should say that Julio Simón—his real name—or Julián the Turk sent me. "Julio Simón, you motherfucker, Julio Simón."

A path leads to the stage where emotions and festivities ebb and flow. A microphone says my name, not my code number but my name. And out of that name springs a voice that resonates despite myself, a voice that stands in front of me determined to speak its own text.

A CERTAIN PERVERSE MAGIC turns the key to the front door. Steps rush in. Three pairs of shoes practice a disjointed stomp on the floor, the clothes, the books, an arm, a hip, an ankle, a hand. My body.

I can almost touch people's eyes as they stare at me, stunned by this voice of mine that repeats

STEP ON A CRACK, break your mother's back

I turn the page; the paper rustles between my fingers. Am I the one who's reading and closing a circle? I'm a tightrope walker trying to keep my balance between present and past, remembrance and fiction:

THEY'RE TAKING me away, they're taking me away!

The secret road between my house and the Athletic Club becomes public, the floodgates open, words spill out. Voices from the past take over my body. I am, we are the poem:

> *murdered*
> *my brother   her son   his grandson*
> *her mother   his girlfriend   her aunt*
> *her grandfather   his friend   his cousin   her neighbor*
> *ours   yours   us*
> *all of us*
> *injected with emptiness.*
> *We lost a version of who we were*
> *and rewrite ourselves in order to survive.*

Words written so my voice can pronounce them here, in this place that is neither dust nor cell but a chorus of voices resisting armed monologues that turned so much life into a single, numberless death.

Glossary

AMIA. The Asociación Mutual Israelita Argentina (Jewish Mutual Aid Association of Argentina). Housed in a building that was subsequently bombed in 1990, resulting in the loss of eighty-six lives. State security forces have been accused of actively participating in this attack.

Club Atlético (Athletic Club). Name given to one of the five largest concentration camps. The others were Vesubio and Campo de Mayo outside Buenos Aires, La Perla in Córdoba, and the ESMA in Buenos Aires itself. Approximately 340 such clandestine prisons, which formed the cornerstone of the military regime, were set up around the country. But even police headquarters were used as torture and illegal detention centers at the time. Camps functioned in rural schools, old tramway warehouses, automobile repair shops, state offices, old provincial radio stations, motels under construction—and the list goes on. Numbers, therefore, cannot give the actual picture of the whole machinery of death.

The Club Atlético was located near the presidential palace. Its official name was Central Antisubversiva (Anti-Subversive Center). The acronym, CA, gave rise to the nickname by which it was commonly known (Andersen, *Dossier Secreto*). Survivors are currently negotiating support for excavations that will uncover the basement of the concentration camp. The proposal is to turn the spot into an open memorial to the victims of genocide.

CONADEP. The Comisión Nacional sobre la Desaparición de Personas (National Commission on Disappeared Persons), established on 15 December 1983 by the first democratically elected government after the dictatorship. Its mandate was to "carry on active investigations in order to clarify the events relating to the forced disappearance of people within the country and to discover their eventual fate and whereabouts, as well as any other information relevant to what happened to them." It was also to "receive formal accusations and proof pertaining to these events, which would then be handed over to the courts if it were found that criminal activity was involved" *(Nunca Más)*. The writer Ernesto Sábato was elected president of the commission. Its final report, *Nunca Más: Never Again,* was based on a selection and analysis of the testimony it gathered.

DAIA. The Delegación de Asociaciones Israelitas Argentinas (Delegation of Jewish Associations of Argentina). Accused of remaining silent during the disappearance of Jewish victims. The Jewish population in Argentina comprises 250,000 out of 34 million, or .735 percent, but it accounted for about 12 percent of the disappeared. Of course, percentages and figures in these cases are approximations.

Dirty War. An expression the Junta used to justify its methods. During the "Dirty War" the United States provided for military training and assistance. Martin Andersen states in *Dossier Secreto* that "the [United States] oriented the Argentine military professionally . . . , exposing them to American technology and methods. The aid offered the chance for improved communication with the Argentine armed forces, which had always influenced events in their country and had now become the dominant sector. This would promote and protect American interests and help ensure that matters of concern to the United States would get a hearing. It was business as usual at Henry Kissinger's State Department" (249).

ESMA. The Escuela de Mecánica de la Armada (School of Navy Mechanics), originally the training center for lower-level officers of the Argentine Navy. Though it was under naval command, other military groups, including the Federal Police and the national prison authority, were also active there. The ESMA began to be used as a covert prison and torture center in May 1976. It was there that intelligence forces planned kidnapping operations, imprisoned those who were brought in, carried out interrogations under torture, and made decisions as to who was to be "transferred." "Transfers" were mass murders in which victims— drugged, but still conscious—were loaded onto military aircraft and then dumped out over the Atlantic Ocean. The Menem government wanted to have the center torn down and replaced with a park and a monument to national unity and reconciliation, a plan adamantly opposed by the Mothers of the Plaza de Mayo, who believe the building should be left intact as a testament to all who disappeared and died there.

Madres de Plaza de Mayo. Organization of mothers of the disappeared that still demands the return of their children and information about what happened to them. For the past quarter-century, from 30 April 1976 until today (although they are divided now into two separate groups), the Madres have met and marched every Thursday afternoon in the Plaza de Mayo, the main square of Buenos Aires and the financial, political, and religious hub of the city. The Junta and the media tried to dismiss them as *locas* (madwomen) during the time of the dictatorship.

Milicos. Pejorative nickname used to refer to military personnel.

Montoneros. A youth organization that formed an incipient guerrilla movement in 1968–69 and then burst onto the Argentine political scene in 1970, gaining increasing popular support. It was the armed wing of the Peronist Youth Movement (Juventud Peronista), and its members identified with the ideals of grass-roots resistance as personified by Eva Perón. They pointed to the revolutionary changes Juan Perón made during the time he ruled with Evita, representing a vision that differed from those of other left-wing organizations of the time.

NN: No name. From the Latin *non nominatus*. Corpses of thousands of *desaparecidos* were buried in mass graves labeled "NN" for anonymity.

El Proceso (The Process). The dictatorship described itself as the Proceso de Reorganización Nacional (Process for National Reorganization). This reorganization was based on the idea that a minority considered by the dictatorship to be subversive and non-Argentine because its ideals clashed with those of Western, Christian traditions had to be expelled from the social body.

Task Forces. Secret detention centers were run by the military, the police, and the Gendarmería (armed border police in rural areas). However, to ensure their clandestine functioning, it was essential to restrict the number of people involved. Consequently, antisubversive operations were placed in the hands of special task forces.

Sources

Archival material was provided by the Center for Legal and Social Studies (CELS), by the Association of Former Detained-Disappeared, and by the National Argentine Commission on Disappeared Persons (CONADEP), all in Buenos Aires, 1985–95.

Andersen, Martin E. *Dossier Secreto: The Myth of the Dirty War.* Boulder: Westview Press, 1993.

Bayer, Osvaldo. *Rebeldía y esperanza* (Rebellion and hope). Madrid: Ediciones B, Grupo Zeta, 1993.

Cortazar, Julio. *Rayuela (Hopscotch).* Buenos Aires: Editorial Sudamericana, 1966.

Gelman, Juan. *Unthinkable Tenderness: Selected Poems / Juan Gelman.* Translated and edited by Joan Lindgren. Berkeley: University of California Press, 1997.

Kaufman, Alejandro. Prologue to *Heidegger y los judíos (Heidegger and the Jews),* by Jean François Lyotard. Buenos Aires: La Marca, 1995.

La sentencia (The sentence). Complete text of the sentence delivered on 9 December 1985 by the Federal Court of Appeals in the national Capitol, Buenos Aires. 2 vols. Buenos Aires: National Congress, 1987.

Martínez, Tomás Eloy. *Lugar común la muerte* (Death as cliché). Caracas: Monte Avila Editores, 1978.

Nunca Más (Never Again): A Report by Argentina's National Commission on Disappeared People. London: Farber, 1986.

Paoletti, Alipio. *Como los nazis, como en Vietnam* (Just like the Nazis, just like in Vietnam). Buenos Aires: Contrapunto, 1987.

Peri Rossi, Cristina. "El club de los amnésicos" (The amnesiac's club), in *Cosmoagonías* (Cosmoagonies). Barcelona: Laia, 1988.

Verbitsky, Horacio. *The Flight: Confessions of an Argentinian Dirty Warrior.* Translated by Esther Allen. New York: New Press, 1996.